Making Your Marriage

Deployment Ready

Mike and Linda Montgomery
Keith and Sharon Morgan

HOMEBUILDERS: MAKING YOUR MARRIAGE DEPLOYMENT READY

PUBLISHED BY FAMILYLIFE PUBLISHING®
5800 Ranch Drive
Little Rock, Arkansas 72223
1-800-FL-TODAY • FamilyLife.com
A ministry of Campus Crusade for Christ, Inc.

Unless otherwise noted, Scripture quotations are from the NEW AMERICAN STANDARD BIBLE®, Copyright © 1960, 1962, 1963, 1968, 1973, 1975, 1977, 1995 by The Lockman Foundation. Used by permission. Scriptures are also cited from the following sources: Scripture quotations indentified NLT are from the Holy Bible, New Living Translation copyright © 1996, 2004 by Tyndale Charitable Trust. Used by permission of Tyndale House Publishers. Scripture quotations indentified as NIV are from the New International Version copyright © 1973, 1978, 1984 by International Bible Society. Used by permission.

ISBN: 978-1-60200-232-6

FamilyLife Publishing® is a registered trademark of FamilyLife, a ministry of Campus Crusade for Christ, Inc.

Graphic Design: Jerome L. Nelson

Printed in the United States of America
2008—First Edition

12 11 10 09 08   1 2 3 4 5

For more information about biblical peacemaking, visit the Peacemaker Ministries Web site at www.Peacemaker.net or contact Peacemaker Ministries at PO Box 81130, Billings, MT 59108 (406/256-1583).

CONTENTS

About the Authors

Mike and Linda Montgomery were high school sweethearts, and have been married since 1970. Twenty-three years were spent moving around the world as an Air Force family until Mike's retirement as a colonel in 1995. They are the parents of two grown, married children, and if asked, are sure to tell you about their grandchildren. Mike and Linda are HomeBuilders directors for the Military Ministry (part of Campus Crusade for Christ) in the Virginia Peninsula, where they live and serve all five branches of the military. Their mission is to train military couples to build strong marriages and leave the lasting legacy of Christian homes.

Keith and Sharon Morgan have been married since 1984. They have two children, Angela and Christina. Keith retired from the Army in 2004, having completed twenty-six years of active duty. He retired as a colonel after serving in a wide variety of command and staff assignments in the United States, Europe, Korea, and southwest Asia. Keith and Sharon have been actively involved in ministry to military couples through HomeBuilders discipleship groups and the Military Marriage Seminar. Keith is currently the director of family ministries for the Military Ministry. The Morgans live in Washington, D.C.

Acknowledgments

This study has truly been a team effort. Since our military life experiences from the Vietnam and Cold War eras are very different from yours, we traveled the country and talked with couples in active duty, Guard, and Reserve units to get a clear and current picture of the challenges faced by today's military families. Along the way, we heard the stories of and witnessed military couples living victorious lives in the face of what the world would say were unreasonably demanding, or even impossible, situations. These couples refuse to be regarded as victims of society or the war on terror, but rather have determined to rise above the circumstances to impact their families, their communities, and their nation. In this HomeBuilders study, we have tried to capture the principles that make their marriages work.

We especially thank the military leaders and chaplains, churches, HomeBuilders groups, and our Military Ministry teams, who worked shoulder to shoulder with us every step of the way. Jim and Lisa Wenschlag, Sid and Connie Thurston, Jim and Bea Fishback, Will Alley, Daryl and Martha Jones, Bob and Dora Sprinkel, Tom and Sue Shillingburg, Mike and Carole Carkhuff, Michael and Aubree

Schnakenberg, and Andy and Stephanie Corbett are special friends who have made significant contributions to the research, structure, and refinement of the study.

The team at FamilyLife, led by Dave Boehi and Rebecca Price, has been gracious in leading us and teaching us throughout the writing and publishing process. We are grateful for their expertise, professionalism, and love for spreading the truth of God's Word.

Finally, we owe our families a debt of gratitude, as they patiently shared the time we spent on the project and faithfully prayed throughout our writing and traveling. They are a blessing beyond compare, and we thank God for them.

Before You Begin: A Word about Deployment

"Sweetheart, I'm going to deploy." Those somber words echo around our country as military couples face the harsh realities of extended and repeated deployments.

As the news of deployment and the reality of separation sink in, many questions arise:

- "How will I manage?"

- "Will my marriage be all right?"

- "Will my family be okay?"

- "Will I be safe?"

- "How do we live apart and stay connected?"

- "Can I manage the children, house, and finances by myself?"

- "How will my spouse cope with loneliness and temptation?"

- "Will we remain faithful while we're separated?"

- "How will our lives change when we're reunited after deployment?"

- "What if the worst happens?"

In other words, people are asking, "Where will I find hope and strength for the trials I will surely experience during the different stages of deployment?"

This study is designed to encourage and equip you with biblical tools that will give you the vision to see through the uncertainties of deployment and will strengthen your marriage. Specifically, we'll address the following topics:

- Identifying deployment tripwires that threaten marriage

- Developing an operational marriage plan for successful deployment

- Implementing principles to stay connected while apart

- Discovering the keys to a strong spiritual foundation

- Smoothing the return home

- Reaching the high ground of a godly legacy

What you will discover as you study these topics is that they are not so much about deployment as about courage, resilience, faith, and honor.

We commend you for investing time and energy in your marriage. Participation in this HomeBuilders Couples Series® study will help you build a stronger relationship with your spouse and develop lasting friendships with other couples.

You and your spouse could complete this study together, just the two of you. However, we urge you to either form or join a group of couples. You will find that the questions in each session help create an environment of warmth and encouragement as you study together to build the type of marriage you desire.

There are only four general rules for HomeBuilders group members:

- Share nothing that would embarrass your spouse.

- You may pass on any question.

- Anything shared in the group stays in the group.

- Complete the HomeBuilders Project with your spouse before the next session.

May God bless you on your journey!

Notes to Group Leaders

1. Leading a group is much easier than you may think. A group leader in a HomeBuilders session is really a facilitator whose goal is simply to guide the group through the discussion questions. You don't need to teach the material—in fact, we don't want you to. The special dynamic of a HomeBuilders group is that couples teach themselves.

2. The *HomeBuilders Discipleship Group Leader's Guide* is a useful tool for hosting and leading a HomeBuilders study. The *HomeBuilders Leader's Guide* is also very practical for learning how to facilitate a study. These resources can be purchased through FamilyLife or Military Ministry.

3. Before each session, refer to appendix E (on page 125), "Leader's Notes," for comments on specific questions in each session.

4. To create a friendly, comfortable atmosphere, we recommend you do this study in a home setting. In many cases, the host couple will also lead the study. Sometimes involving another couple to host is a good idea. Choose whatever option you feel will work best for your group, taking into account factors such as the number of couples participating and the location.

5. The material presented in each session is designed for a ninety-minute study; however, we recommend scheduling a two-hour block of time. This will allow you to move through each part of the study at a relaxed pace and still have time for fellowship and refreshments.

6. It is important to start and end your sessions on time. Also, it is key for couples to commit to attending all the sessions and completing each of the HomeBuilders Projects.

7. If you are about to deploy or are currently deployed, consider using instant messaging (IM) or Webcam to continue the HomeBuilders study and stay connected with your spouse and/or group.

8. This study is unlike any other HomeBuilders study in that it concludes with a commitment ceremony in session 6. An engraved Commitment Certificate, suitable for framing, and the Commitment Coin, which comes in a gift case, are available for purchase from the Military Ministry online store at *http://resources.MilitaryMinistry.org*. See appendix B for further details on page 111.

A Letter from Dennis Rainey and Bob Dees

Dear Military Couples,

Deployment and reintegration may be the biggest challenge you will encounter in your marriage over the course of your military career. The busy operational tempo of today's military lifestyle will add stress, tension, doubt, and uncertainty to many couples' lives.

Couples may find themselves at risk if they're unprepared or ill-equipped for what lies ahead. The pressures that deployment and reintegration bring may shake the foundation of commitment, love, and teamwork in a marriage.

Making Your Marriage Deployment Ready is designed to bring hope and victory to couples facing these challenges. This study incorporates time-tested principles and applies them to the military lifestyle. You'll find the study easy to use and practical for your marriage.

Psalm 127:1a says, "Unless the Lord builds the house, they labor in vain who build it." This study, part of the HomeBuilders Couples Series, will help you apply biblical truths to your marriage. You will learn them in an encouraging environment along with other couples who face the same pressures in marriage.

We hope this will be a life-changing tool to help you build a marriage that will go the distance for a lifetime ... to have the marriage you always wanted. May this small-group experience called HomeBuilders be one of the very best experiences of your life!

Yours for building strong military families,

Dennis Rainey
President, FamilyLife

Robert F. Dees
Major General, U.S. Army (Retired)
Executive Director, Military Ministry

SUPREME HEADQUARTERS
ALLIED EXPEDITIONARY FORCE

Soldiers, Sailors and Airmen of the Allied Expeditionary Force!

You are about to embark upon the Great Crusade, toward which we have striven these many months.   The eyes of the world are upon you. The hopes and prayers of liberty-loving people everywhere march with you. In company with our brave Allies and brothers-in-arms on other Fronts, you will bring about the destruction of the German war machine, the elimination of Nazi tyranny over the oppressed peoples of Europe, and security for ourselves in a free world.

Your task will not be an easy one.   Your enemy is well trained, well equipped and battle-hardened.   He will fight savagely.

But this is the year 1944 ! Much has happened since the Nazi triumphs of 1940-41. The United Nations have inflicted upon the Germans great defeats, in open battle, man-to-man.   Our air offensive has seriously reduced their strength in the air and their capacity to wage war on the ground.   Our Home Fronts have given us an overwhelming superiority in weapons and munitions of war, and placed at our disposal great reserves of trained fighting men.   The tide has turned ! The free men of the world are marching together to Victory !

I have full confidence in your courage, devotion to duty and skill in battle.   We will accept nothing less than full Victory !

Good Luck !   And let us all beseech the blessing of Almighty God upon this great and noble undertaking.

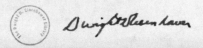

Deployment Threats

A military couple can successfully face
deployment by working together to avoid the
minefields of unintended consequences.

History Nugget

On the eve of the D-Day invasion in June 1944,
Supreme Allied Commander Dwight D. Eisenhower
delivered this now-famous letter (image on facing
page) to the soldiers, sailors, and airmen of the
Allied Expeditionary Force.[1] The tone inspired
greatness in all who read it. Absolute and total
victory was the only option. This same courage,
devotion to duty, and resilient attitude will result in
a world-changing victory in our marriages as well.

WARM•UP   15   MINUTES

1. Each couple should introduce themselves to the
group. In less than two minutes, tell how you met
and what attracted you to your spouse.

2. Tell the group how many times you've relocated in the military and which assignment you have enjoyed the most.

3. The military lifestyle is a busy, stressful one. What do you like to do for fun or relaxation?

BLUEPRINTS   60 MINUTES

It is healthy to remind yourself just why you got married in the first place—what really attracted you to your spouse. It's safe to say that no couple exchanges vows on their wedding day thinking their marriage is going to fail! The same applies to a couple facing a deployment. No one plans to fail.

Just like planning for a military mission, we must be realistic about the threats we could encounter along the way. It can be scary, but there is hope in this journey.

CASE STUDY

Al and Maria are young newlyweds in the military who moved into the home next door a few months ago. Everything is new to this young couple—being away from home, learning to depend on one another—all complicated by the fact that this is their first duty assignment.

Al came home today with some shocking news: Their unit has orders to deploy! Al and Maria knew deployment was a significant part of military life, but they really hadn't expected it to come quite so soon.

Maria is understandably worried about Al's safety, as there is an element of danger in any military assignment.

You and your spouse have been through several deployments, and you know there are other pressures and problems this young couple will face during deployment—challenges they don't seem to even be aware of.

1. What would you tell Al and Maria about the challenges they are likely to face during deployment?

2. Do you believe that the challenges of deployment cause problems—or merely reveal problems?

Recent history has shown that many military couples are not prepared for the pressures and challenges they face before, during, and after deployment. As you consider your next deployment, you would be wise to consider three threats to your marriage relationship: uncertainties and difficult adjustments, selfishness, and poor communication. These are a challenge in normal circumstances, but in a deployment these threats are magnified.

Threat #1: Uncertainties and Difficult Adjustments

Although all couples face changes based on their family history, roles, seasons of life, and expectations, deployment brings its own set of challenging adjustments.

3. Looking back at the Case Study, what adjustments will Al and Maria need to make before, during, and after deployment?

4. How will their attitudes affect their reaction to these changes in their lives?

Threat #2: Selfishness

Merriam-Webster Collegiate Dictionary, 10th edition, defines *selfish* as being "concerned excessively or exclusively with oneself; seeking or concentrating on one's own advantage, pleasure, or well-being without regard for others." We can all be that way at times, as we are naturally self-centered creatures and want to have things our way.

5. It is sometimes easier to see selfishness in someone else than in yourself. Why do you think this is true?

6. In what ways can deployment make it easier to focus on yourself than on your spouse?

7. Philippians 2:3–4 tells us:

Do nothing out of selfish ambition or vain

*conceit, but in humility consider others better
than yourselves. Each of you should look not only
to your own interests, but also to the interests of
others.* (NIV)

What are some ways you can apply this verse and
think of your spouse more than yourself during the
separation of a deployment?

Threat #3: Poor Communication

Good communication between a husband and
a wife can make a marriage. By communicating
information clearly, sharing hopes and
desires, giving opinions, and responding with
encouragement, you build connections in your
relationship.

8. What are some differences in the way you and
your spouse communicate?

9. What challenges do you expect in maintaining
communication during deployment?

10. What changes could you make to improve your
communication before deployment?

In order to address the threats to a marriage during deployment, it helps to look at God's purposes for marriage. Genesis 2:24 tells us, "For this reason a man will leave his father and mother and be united to his wife, and they will become one flesh" (NIV). We will look more closely at this verse in the next session, but notice how it speaks of the priority of the marriage relationship: It is more important than the bond between you and your parents, and it involves two people becoming one.

1. If you want your marriage to be a priority, how can you communicate that to your spouse?

2. If you are totally committed to your spouse and to making your marriage work, how will that affect you as you deal with a deployment?

> **HomeBuilders Principle**
> *An absolute commitment to making your marriage work for a lifetime will allow your relationship to endure the threats of a deployment.*

Get Connected

Circulate a sign-up sheet for couples to share their names, phone numbers, and e-mail addresses with the group.

Make a Date

Make a date for you and your spouse to go through your HomeBuilders Project before the next group session.

_____
DATE

_____
TIME

_____
LOCATION

_____

Couple's Azimuth Check (10 minutes)

Anyone experienced in navigation—whether on
land, sea, or air—can appreciate how critical it is
to hold a precise magnetic heading, or azimuth.
One degree doesn't seem like a lot, but if you stray
one degree off the planned heading over a 60-mile
course, you will miss your desired destination by
a mile! The same concept applies to marriage. If
you and your spouse don't have a "fix" on the same
objective (destination), or if you are not on the same
"azimuth," you will soon find you have drifted miles
apart. Use this self-assessment tool throughout this
study to see just how close the two of you are to
being on the same azimuth with your marriage.

During the group session, we discussed three
threats to a marriage: uncertainties and difficult
adjustments, selfishness, and poor communication.
To gain insight into how much the three threats
have affected your marriage, please rate them by
circling the appropriate number (1 being the least
significant and 5 the most significant). Describe

the impact the threat has had on your marriage in general and then describe the impact this threat has had or could have on your marriage during deployment.

THREAT	SIGNIFICANCE	IMPACT*
Uncertainties and difficult adjustments	1 2 3 4 5	
Selfishness	1 2 3 4 5	
Poor com- munication	1 2 3 4 5	

*IMPACT on your marriage in general and on your marriage during deployment

Individually (15 minutes)

1. What is the main thing you learned during the group session?

2. Look through the following list and put a check by any of the ways you often deal with stress in your life … and in your marriage.

___ exercise

___ keep a prayer journal

___ work harder

___ go shopping

___ talk on the telephone

___ spend more time on TV, Internet, or video games

___ deny any problems

___ become preoccupied with a hobby

___ tough it out

___ seek to learn new skills

___ sleep more (or less)

___ eat more (or less)

___ withdraw from friends

___ get bitter and/or angry

___ drink to excess or smoke

___ find someone else to help—one who shares your circumstances

___ turn to good influences for support

___ other: _____

___ other: _____

3. How successful are these methods in dealing with stress?

Interact as a Couple (25 minutes)

4. Share your answers from the individual section above.

5. If this is your family's first deployment, what issues do you think you need to face as you prepare for deployment?

6. If you've experienced deployment, look back at the impact the deployment(s) had on your marriage. What would you change about how the two of you handled the deployment?

7. Review the History Nugget on page 1. What did General Eisenhower's D-Day message to his troops say that encourages you in this deployment?

For Extra Impact (10 minutes)

CASE STUDY

Charles and Jennifer have been in the military all their married life. They have experienced multiple deployments, and their marriage seems pretty solid. But Jennifer had not been prepared for the discussion they had several years ago as they prepared for one of those deployments.

Charles told Jennifer, "The military is more than a job for me—it's my calling." His intensity and emotion surprised her as he described his commitment to the service, the nation, and the responsibility he felt for the men and women entrusted to him to lead into harm's way.

And then he added, "I need you to share my calling."

Jennifer's mind raced back across their eleven years of marriage. She thought she had been supportive of his career. After all, hadn't she smiled adoringly at him as they attended countless functions? Hadn't she made a lovely, peaceful home at each and every duty station? Wasn't all that enough? What else did he need from her?

Have you ever considered your military service as a "calling"?

A calling is defined as "an objective or task that somebody believes is his or her duty to carry out or to which he or she attaches special importance and devotes special care." [2]

Accordingly, a professional calling goes beyond earning a living; it connotes a passion. When we view military service as a joint calling it alters our view of circumstances and challenges. Sharing a passion gives rise to a vision of something greater—a new and different approach to life in the military.

8. At this point in your marriage, would you say you have a "shared calling" to the military? Is that something you've even thought about?

9. If you were to have a shared calling, how do you think that would affect the way you view deployment?

Recommended Resources

Covenant Marriage: Building Communication and Intimacy, by Gary D. Chapman

Hope for the Home Front: Winning the Emotional and Spiritual Battles of a Military Wife, by Marshele Carter Waddell

Love and Respect: The Love She Most Desires, the Respect He Desperately Needs, by Emerson Eggerichs

On the Frontline: A Personal Guidebook for the Physical, Emotional, and Spiritual Challenges of Military Life, by Tom Neven

Sacred Marriage, by Gary L. Thomas

Strike the Original Match, by Charles R. Swindoll

Mission Planning

Military couples should establish and implement
a deployment plan for their marriage.

History Nugget

*Your letter was a treat to me. The expressions
of affection, and the accompanying prayers for
me, are grateful to the heart. You expect us to
move forward very soon, either to another great
battle on our own soil, or to invade that of our
enemies. Of course, I cannot tell what a day may
bring forth, but I see no reason to expect a great
battle so soon. I am ready, I hope, for anything.
I do not feel like turning my face homeward,
however, until all at home are relieved from fear
of the enemy. I wish to return to enjoy with you
the pleasures of home in peace, and not to share
the anxieties which now distress you. Let us only
bear up with Christian firmness, and fight with
courage, trusting in God, and we may hope for a
speedy close to the war.*[1]

—A letter from a Confederate soldier
to his mother, March 1862

1. Share something you and your spouse learned from the HomeBuilders Project.

2. We all make plans for important times in our lives—weddings, trips, moves, holidays. What are some special plans you have made as a couple?

3. Reflect on the Civil War soldier's letter. What differences in planning can you imagine it required to leave home for that war?

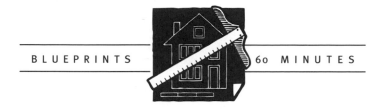

CASE STUDY

Maria gets to hear another perspective on deployment planning from Jackie, one of the other wives in the unit. Jackie and her husband, Robert, are a unique couple, as both of them are on active duty. While Jackie will be a part of this deployment, Robert's assignment will keep him at home with their two children. Despite the fact that this is not Jackie and Robert's first deployment, they are still struggling with the logistics of the family and trying to work out the details of child care and contingencies for the kids. Even though both are known for professional competence, these family issues have been very challenging, as they require extra flexibility on the part of both in their roles.

Maria comments, "Our situation is different, since Al is the one who is deploying and I will be home alone. The problem now is that we don't seem to be on the same page. I just want to spend what precious time we have left together, but he is really focused on his unit deployment checklist. His mind seems to be elsewhere."

1. In what ways can you relate to the situations these two couples find themselves in?

- If you have been deployed, how well did you prepare for your first deployment?

- If you have been on multiple deployments, how did you find the planning process on subsequent deployments? Did you apply lessons you had learned, or had your family's circumstances changed significantly?

A unit deployment will not be successful without a detailed deployment plan. Provisions under the plan will typically include individual and small-unit training, equipment maintenance and preparation, team building and communication exercises, contingency operations, and a time-phased movement plan to get the unit there with everything it needs.

If the family is the most important "unit" in God's eyes, then it needs a plan, too. The challenge then becomes how to be as professional, thorough, and focused on the family plan as we are on implementing the unit's pre-deployment plan.

Mission Planning

There are numerous passages in Scripture about planning. Here are two significant ones:

Plans fail for lack of counsel, but with many advisers they succeed.

—Proverbs 15:22 NIV

Whoever gives heed to instruction prospers, and blessed is he who trusts in the LORD.

—Proverbs 16:20 NIV

2. How could we apply the truths of these passages to planning in a marriage?

3. Why is it difficult to plan for a deployment? What are some of the distractions couples face in getting ready?

4. What is the value of getting advice when making plans? Whom should we seek out for advice?

5. List the subjects you need to discuss in order to

create a successful deployment plan. (You will be doing this in your project time.)

God's Plan for Oneness in Marriage

Since God created man and woman and the institution of marriage, it should be no surprise He had a plan. God's plan provides for oneness—the spiritual, emotional, and physical uniting of a husband and a wife. There are three phases to God's plan, as outlined in Genesis 2:24 (NIV): "For this reason a man will leave his father and mother, and be united to his wife, and they will become one flesh."

Phase 1: Leave.

6. What do you believe is meant by "leaving" your father and mother? Why is this important in a marriage?

Phase 2: Be united.

7. What does it mean to "be united" in a marriage?

8. How can you tell if a couple is united in their relationship, or if they are acting independently of each other?

9. How can deployment lead to independence in a marriage? How can you use it to build interdependence instead?

Phase 3: Be intimate.

Becoming one flesh is more than a physical act. Rather, this physical union is an expression of oneness with the total person—uniting spirit, soul, and body.

10. What are some things a couple can do to build emotional and spiritual intimacy in their marriage? How could a couple work these things into a deployment plan?

11. What do the following Scripture passages tell us about sexual temptation?

Proverbs 6:32

1 Thessalonians 4:3–8

1 Corinthians 6:18–20

12. Intimacy in marriage can be destroyed by infidelity, often in the form of pornography or adultery. In what ways can a spouse (either the one deployed or the one at home) be sexually tempted during a deployment? What protective measures can be taken to avoid these temptations?

WRAP•UP   15 MINUTES

As a couple, pick one of the following three questions to answer. Then share your answer with the group.

• How can deployments increase our dependence on one another?

- In what ways can deployments enhance our feelings of intimacy for one another?

- What is one way that deployment can affect our relationship with our parents?

HomeBuilders Principle
Establishing and implementing a deployment plan will help strengthen your marriage.

Make a Date

Our date is scheduled for—

DATE

TIME

LOCATION

Couple's Azimuth Check (10 minutes)

1. How does each of you react when plans change? Do you pout, stuff your feelings, explode, or understand the need to be flexible?

2. Read Proverbs 19:21 together. What does it mean to you as a couple?

Individually (10 minutes)

3. During deployment, what people, places, and behaviors could threaten your trust, commitment, and oneness with your spouse?

4. How can you avoid those temptations? How can you help each other avoid these temptations?

5. Consider seeking help from someone who could hold you accountable. Whom would that be?

Interact as a Couple (40 minutes)

6. Create a deployment plan. Discuss each of the following topics. Once you are in agreement, write an action statement for how you will manage each area in your time of separation.

- Budget (Remember to include how you will use combat-area pay and tax benefits, as well as passwords for accounts.)

- Bill paying (Who pays? Which accounts? Any special instructions?)

- Legal documents (Wills, powers of attorney)

- Allotments and savings (Do you have a special file with account information and passwords?)

- Home and car maintenance (Whom does the at-home spouse call for help?)

- Mid-tour R&R (Where? Immediate family only, or do you include parents? Who is going to tell them?)

- Birthday, anniversary, and Christmas gifts (Can you shop ahead of time?)

- Children—including their discipline (Any issues with school or friends? Special vacations or trips? Whom can you rely on for child care in case of emergency?)

- Support groups (Whom do both of you rely on?)

- Emergencies (Perhaps a weather-related evacuation, emergency contact numbers posted in a prominent place)

- Church/chapel involvement (Which chapel/church, and where? Are you in agreement on classes and programs for the kids?)

- Reunion and reintegration (Homecoming with the extended family, or time alone?)

- Accountability partners (Make sure they are people you both respect and are of the same gender.)

- Dealing with in-laws (Who will be responsible for communicating with them?)

- Recreational activities (Enough for relaxation, but not so much as to avoid responsibilities)

- Prayer (How can you support each other through prayer? Getting into the discipline of praying for and with each other now will strengthen your marriage throughout this deployment.)

- Insurance policies (Where are they? Are your beneficiaries current?)

- Computer (To whom does the at-home spouse go for help? How about all those passwords?)

- Other

For Extra Impact

In case of death—things to consider:

Some couples may prefer to skip this section, but those who have been through the death of a spouse strongly recommend that every couple take the necessary time to prepare for the worst. Talking about this difficult topic can help couples better prepare for deployment.

> *Thankfully, my husband and I had "the talk" before his second deployment. Because of this discussion, which was very difficult, I knew what decisions to make when the time came. The result for me was peace.*
>
> —A Gold Star widow

You may want to use this page to jot down planning ideas, or use the questions as a springboard for discussion. This exercise is intended for both spouses.

1. Where do you want to be buried and who will take care of the funeral arrangements?

2. Are there any ideas for your funeral service you want me to know about? For example: pallbearers, which church, whom to officiate, favorite music?

3. Do you have a preference for where you want our family to settle?

4. What is your opinion on remarriage?

5. What are your hopes and dreams for the children?

6. Consider writing a personal letter to each family member before the deployment, a letter to be read in case of your death.

7. How do you want to be remembered?

Recommended Resources

Torn Asunder: Recovering from an Extramarital Affair, by Dave Carder

The Enticement of the Forbidden: Protecting Your Marriage, by Judy Starr

Every Man's Battle: Winning the War on Sexual Temptation One Victory at a Time, by Stephen Arterburn, Fred Stoeker, and Mike Yorkey

Every Woman's Battle: Discovering God's Plan for Sexual and Emotional Fulfillment, by Shannon Ethridge and Stephen Arterburn

Footsteps of the Faithful: Victorious Living and the Military Life, by Denise McColl

Heroes at Home: Help and Hope for America's Military Families, by Ellie Kay

Military Widow: A Survival Guide, by Joanne M. Steen and M. Regina Asaro

Separated by Duty, United in Love, by Shellie Vandevoorde

Staying Connected with Each Other

Genuine communication strengthens trust, commitment, and oneness in a military marriage.

History Nugget

Darling ... Theresa, dear, why don't you write me sometime more intimately about yourself, what your opinion on things is, what you think about, what your interests are, anything at all so that I can feel I am closer to you when I read your letters, something that will reveal you yourself, in all your charm and sweetness, just say anything at all as long as it concerns you and I will love it ... [1]

—From a letter dated April 3, 1933, from Chaplain Alexander Goode to his sweetheart, Theresa

1. Take a few minutes to share with the group something funny about your courtship days.

2. Cards, letters, and gifts are often exchanged during our courtship days. How did they serve to enhance your relationship? Feel free to share a treasured memory with the group.

3. Share something you learned from the last HomeBuilders Project.

CASE STUDY

As the deployment preparation continues, you invite Al and Maria over for dinner periodically. On one occasion you include your mutual friends, Robert and Jackie.

As the guys sit around before dinner, it doesn't take long for the conversation to drift into deployment planning. Al admits that he and Maria are trying to be sensitive to each other's needs as they do their planning, but it isn't easy.

Then Robert admits, "Our struggle in the last deployment was with communication. Jackie saw this first, and she brought it to my attention. We realized we had issues, but we weren't talking, and there was bitterness over it. Our lack of forgiveness led to a state of isolation. It wasn't pretty, and it didn't get any better when I returned home."

1. What advice would you give Al about what he should do to maintain communication with Maria over the course of the deployment?

2. If you've been on a deployment: How would you evaluate your communication while you were apart? What did you do well, and what could be improved?

3. Read the History Nugget. What advice would Chaplain Goode give regarding communication during deployment(s)?

It has been said a commitment to marriage is a commitment to communicate. Because of the geographic separation in deployments, staying connected is even more important and more of a challenge. A couple must be creative and intentional—and willing to share at the heart level—in order to finish the deployment strong.

4. Our key Scripture verse in this session is James 1:19:

> *Everyone should be quick to listen, slow to speak and slow to become angry* (NIV).

We can find three communication skills in this verse. What do you think is the meaning of each of the following phrases?

- "quick to listen"

- "slow to speak"

- "slow to become angry"

When we find ourselves in difficult situations, our natural tendency is often to respond with the opposite approach: we are slow to listen, quick to speak, and quick to become angry. And deployment may be one of the most difficult situations a couple can face in marriage.

Skill #1: Listening

Ask good questions
that show interest, concern, and love

Listen to what your spouse says

Show interest in what your spouse says

Keys to Listening:
Understanding your spouse's needs and interests.

5. In a conversation, do you find listening easy or difficult? Why?

6. During a deployment, how can a couple maintain an interest in each other's lives?

7. How do good questions open up communication? How can assumptions, sarcasm, or demands stifle it?

8. Look at the following statements. How can you change these statements into questions that could encourage your spouse to talk and share more deeply with you?

> "I hope you had a good day today."
>
> "Tell me the family news."
>
> "I guess the kids are doing fine at school."
>
> *If you know what means something to each family member, you'll be able to communicate with him or her more effectively while you're away.*[2]
>
> —Carol Vandesteeg, *When Duty Calls*

Skill #2: Expressing

Communication is a lot like tennis. One person begins the conversation by making a statement, and then perhaps asking a question—like serving the ball. The other person returns the ball by responding to the statement and/or question, and perhaps asks another question. And so the game continues.

Like tennis, good communication takes practice. This includes conversation. If all you can contribute are clichés or facts, then you are not sharing very deeply. Couples who can talk about what they think and feel without becoming defensive or being threatened by rejection are couples who can weather a tough situation together. The purpose of communication in marriage is to stay connected. Barriers to communication will only produce isolation—especially during a deployment.

9. If you've been deployed before, which methods of communication do you prefer: e-mail, IM, Webcam, letters, or phone calls? Which ones does your spouse prefer?

10. It's easier to communicate at a "fact level" (sharing information) than staying connected at the heart level (sharing feelings). During deployment, how can you move to this deeper heart level of communication?

> *Modern communication technology can make a bad marriage worse and a good marriage better.*
>
> —A very experienced chaplain

Skill #3: Dealing with Conflict

This may surprise you, but all marriages have

conflict. Therefore, understanding conflict and learning to resolve differences are important steps in strengthening any marriage.

11. Why are misunderstandings more likely to happen during a deployment? What can you do to avoid them?

12. Read Colossians 3:13:

Bear with each other and forgive whatever grievances you may have against one another. Forgive as the Lord forgave you. (NIV)

What does it mean to forgive each other "as the Lord forgave you"? If you can, share about a time when forgiveness was a key part in resolving a conflict.

13. How can it be more difficult to seek and grant forgiveness during deployment?

Answer these questions with your spouse and share your answers with the group:

1. How can resolving conflict actually serve to strengthen marriage?

2. Why would it be important to properly address unresolved issues prior to deployment?

HomeBuilders Principle

Communication is an essential aspect of marriage, because everything else depends on it, especially during a deployment.

Make a Date

Our date is scheduled for—

_____
DATE

_____
TIME

_____
LOCATION

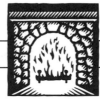

HOMEBUILDERS PROJECT   60   M I N U T E S

Couple's Azimuth Check (15 minutes)

Answer the following questions:

1. How well have we done in communicating with each other in the past, especially during deployment(s)?

2. In what ways can we improve?

Individually (15 minutes)

3. Take fifteen minutes to write a letter of appreciation to your spouse that she or he can read for encouragement during the deployment. Write it as if you are speaking and your spouse is listening. In this letter, include the things that attracted you to your spouse, what you appreciate about her or him in your marriage, how you have grown in your understanding of yourself and your spouse since you have been married, and what you plan to do to demonstrate commitment to your spouse and to the growth of your marriage. Put this letter in a safe place. You will return to it at the end of session 5.

Interact as a Couple (30 minutes)

Develop a "Communication Annex" for your deployment using the following table as an outline. Remember, based on location or resources, not all these means of communication will be available to all couples. Additionally, you might want to keep some of the suggestions secret. A surprise is always appreciated. The list is meant to give you ideas. Be creative.[3]

Means of Corresponding	Deployed Spouse	At-Home Spouse	Frequency
Phone calls			
E-mails			
Letters			
Letters left with friends			
Working through a devotional or using an online devotional together			
Reading a book together			
Cards or gifts left with friends for key dates (birthdays, anniversary, etc.)			
Small gifts or flowers			
Notes inside luggage or hidden at home			
Pictures displayed so others will see them			
CDs or DVDs to each other			
Webcam calls			
Prayer			
Other:			

For Extra Impact

Resolving conflict requires loving confrontation. The following two tables provide a simple framework you might find helpful in addressing recurring or unresolved conflicts. The first table talks about how to focus your discussion, while the second, "The Seven A's of Confession," provides a step-by-step checklist to help you keep your communication progressing.

If you have an unresolved or recurring conflict where you have hurt your spouse, write it down on a separate piece of paper. Schedule a time before the next group meeting to come together in an attitude of love and forgiveness to discuss that hurt using these tables as a guide.[4]

FOCUS ON:	RATHER THAN:
One issue	Many issues
The problem	The person
Behavior	Character
Specifics	Generalizations
Expression of feelings	Judgment of character
"I" statements	"You" statements
Observation of facts	Judgment of motive
Mutual understanding	Who's winning or losing

A loving confrontation can lead to forgiveness and reconciliation:

THE SEVEN A's OF CONFESSION[5]	
Address…	everyone involved (Proverbs 28:13; John 1:8–9)
Avoid…	if, but, and maybe (don't make excuses; Luke 15:11–24)
Admit…	specifically (both attitudes and actions)
Apologize…	by expressing sorrow for the way you affected someone
Accept…	the consequences
Alter…	your behavior (commit to changing harmful habits; Ephesians 4:22–32)
Ask…	for forgiveness

© Peacemaker Ministries. Used by permission.

Do not repay evil with evil or insult with insult, but with blessing, because to this you were called so that you may inherit a blessing.

—1 Peter 3:9 NIV

Recommended Resources

Cracking the Communication Code: The Secret to Speaking Your Mate's Language, by Emerson Eggerichs

Deployed, Not Disconnected, edited by Karen and Don Martin Jr.

Fight Fair! Winning at Conflict Without Losing at Love, by Tim and Joy Downs

The Five Love Languages: How to Express Heartfelt Commitment to Your Mate, by Gary Chapman

For Men Only: A Straightforward Guide to the Inner Lives of Women, by Shaunti and Jeff Feldhahn

For Women Only: What You Need to Know About the Inner Lives of Men, by Shaunti Feldhahn

Love Talks for Couples, by Gary Chapman and Ramon Presson

Improving Communication in Your Marriage, by Gary and Barbara Rosberg. This study is one of FamilyLife's HomeBuilders Couples Series for small-group studies.

ExcellentOrPraiseworthy.org, an online devotional by Military Ministry

Thriving During Deployment

Being faithful and committed to and supportive of one another, in the power of God, will enable you to thrive in the midst of deployment and reintegration.

History Nugget

If by some miracle of God I survived this situation, I would go home to my family. As a Christian I also knew if I died I'd go home to heaven and be with my Savior. So no matter what happens to me tonight, I'm going home. I'm going to be safe, I thought. From that moment on, I felt no fear.[1]

—Sergeant Jeff Struecker, about his experience with Task Force Ranger in Somalia

1. Share something you learned from your HomeBuilders Project.

2. As a child, did you have any fictional heroes you admired? For example, comic action heroes like Superman, Wonder Woman, or Spiderman? Or movie heroes like Indiana Jones or James Bond? What qualities did you admire in these heroes?

3. What qualities do these heroes typically demonstrate when facing adversity?

CASE STUDY

You are talking with another couple, Steve and Tonya, about their experience during his initial deployment. Steve weighs his words carefully: "Tonya and I had some struggles and disappointments the first go. What hurt the most was that our whole mindset was just to survive the months I was gone, and it was like we put our lives on hold. Neither of us really grew personally or spiritually. We felt our lack of growth meant that we had wasted a significant opportunity for maturing."

Tonya enters the conversation at this point. "You often see couples who are just marking time. You'll hear them say, 'Well, when we get through this deployment …' or 'When we get to the next assignment, then we can start living again.'"

"Now we're facing another deployment," Tonya continues. "And we've decided we don't want to just survive. We want to thrive!"

1. What ideas do you have for ways Steve and Tonya could thrive as individuals and as a married couple during their deployment?

Choosing Your Attitude

Our attitude is developed by our pattern of thinking over time. A good attitude can serve us well when we are confronted by a challenge. A bad attitude can harm us, because negative thinking can cause us to become discouraged and without hope. Although we have little control over our circumstances, we *can* control our attitude about our circumstances.

2. In order to have a proper attitude, what do you have to do with your thinking? What do the following verses have to say about our minds?

> *And do not be conformed to this world, but be transformed by the renewing of your mind, so that you may prove what the will of God is, that which is good and acceptable and perfect.*
>
> —Romans 12:2

Set your mind on the things above, not on the things that are on earth.

—Colossians 3:2

Finally, brethren, whatever is true, whatever is honorable, whatever is right, whatever is pure, whatever is lovely, whatever is of good repute, if there is any excellence and if anything worthy of praise, dwell on these things.

—Philippians 4:8

3. What are some positive or negative attitudes we can have about deployment? What are the potential consequences of those attitudes? If you can, share your experience of how positive or negative attitudes affected you during deployment.

4. What influences can you choose that would help you have a positive attitude? What influences must you avoid?

We must give up this victim mentality. Being negative about deployment doesn't help me any, it doesn't help the kids any, and it sure doesn't help him any! I am determined to finish well.

—Wife of an active duty soldier

This military wife was making the choice to not just survive the deployment, but to thrive. Moving from the attitude of a victim to the attitude of stewardship will cause one to ask, "How can I use this deployment to serve and honor God?"

Five Keys to Thriving During Deployment

It's been noted that couples choosing to thrive during deployment will need to address at least five key areas of their lives:

Key #1: Couples who thrive are growing.

5. How can the time of separation during deployment be a special time for personal growth? What does Philippians 4:11–13 advise?

Not that I speak from want, for I have learned to be content in whatever circumstances I am. I know how to get along with humble means, and

I also know how to live in prosperity; in any and every circumstance I have learned the secret of being filled and going hungry, both of having abundance and suffering need. I can do all things through Him who strengthens me.

Key #2: Couples who thrive are in a community.

6. What does the following passage say about the value of being part of a church or chapel community?

Let us hold fast the confession of our hope without wavering, for He who promised is faithful; and let us consider how to stimulate one another to love and good deeds, not forsaking our own assembling together, as is the habit of some, but encouraging one another; and all the more as you see the day drawing near.

—Hebrews 10:23–25

7. What groups will it be helpful for you to join during this deployment—whether you are the one deployed or the one who stays home?

8. How can you avoid the temptation to be part of groups that will not be helpful?

Key #3: Couples who thrive have faith in God.

9. Proverbs 3:5–6 tells us, "Trust in the Lord with all your heart, and do not lean on your own understanding. In all your ways acknowledge Him, and He will make your paths straight." What qualities have you observed in the lives of married couples who demonstrate a strong faith? How can you make these qualities part of your relationship?

Key #4: Couples who thrive understand that God is in control.

10. What do the following Scripture passages say about who is in charge? How can this knowledge help you through circumstances such as a deployment?

> *"As for you, you meant evil against me, but God meant it for good in order to bring about this present result, to preserve many people alive."*
>
> —Genesis 50:20

But now, thus says the LORD, your Creator, O Jacob, and He who formed you, O Israel, "Do not fear, for I have redeemed you; I have called you by name; you are Mine! When you pass through the waters, I will be with you; and through the rivers, they will not overflow you. When you walk through the fire, you will not be scorched, nor will the flame burn you. For I am the LORD your God, the Holy One of Israel, your Savior."

—Isaiah 43:1–3

And we know that God causes all things to work together for good to those who love God, to those who are called according to His purpose.

—Romans 8:28

W R A P • U P   15   M I N U T E S

Key #5: Couples who thrive make God the anchor of their lives.

Many married people rely heavily on their spouses for security and happiness. Our observation has been that couples who thrive during a deployment are those who have made God the anchor of their life together.

Read Deuteronomy 30:19–20a (NLT):

> *Today I have given you the choice between life and death, between blessings and curses. Now I call on heaven and earth to witness the choice you make. Oh, that you would choose life, so that you and your descendants might live! You can make this choice by loving the LORD your God, obeying him, and committing yourself firmly to him. This is the key to your life.*

Answer these questions with your spouse and then share your answers with the group:

1. In what ways does choosing to walk in God's ways lead to "really living"?

In session 1, we named three threats to oneness that can occur because of a deployment. Understanding the reality of what we are facing while geographically separated, how can staying anchored to God help us face:

- Uncertainties and difficult adjustments?

- Selfishness?

- Communication challenges?

Making the choice to be anchored to God is possible because He wants to have a relationship with us, and because He made it possible through His Son, Jesus Christ. If you want to learn more about how you can experience God's love, peace, and forgiveness through a relationship with Him, turn to appendix A on page 103.

HomeBuilders Principle
Choosing to thrive during deployment can yield long-lasting benefits in your marriage.

Make a Date

Our date is scheduled for—

_____
DATE

_____
TIME

_____
LOCATION
_____

Individually (20 minutes)

In any situation, we can choose to respond negatively or positively. These choices often present themselves in different forms, some of which are represented in the following table.

1. Circle the number to indicate how you have done in the past in terms of your choices in these areas.

Quitting	**1**	**2**	**3**	**4**	**5**	Persevering (James 1:12)
Yielding to temptation	**1**	**2**	**3**	**4**	**5**	Exhibiting self-control (Galatians 5:22–24)
Complaining	**1**	**2**	**3**	**4**	**5**	Being content (Philippians 4:11–13)
Withdrawing	**1**	**2**	**3**	**4**	**5**	Seeking fellowship (Hebrews 10:25)
Yielding to cultural temptations	**1**	**2**	**3**	**4**	**5**	Seeking purity (1 John 2:15–17)
Losing perspective	**1**	**2**	**3**	**4**	**5**	Keeping perspective (James 4:14)
Fearing the worst	**1**	**2**	**3**	**4**	**5**	Keeping the faith (1 Timothy 6:12)
Worrying	**1**	**2**	**3**	**4**	**5**	Remaining confident in the face of adversity (Romans 8:37–39)
Doubting	**1**	**2**	**3**	**4**	**5**	Trusting (Proverbs 3:5–6)
Panicking	**1**	**2**	**3**	**4**	**5**	Remaining calm (Philippians 4:6–7)
Overspending	**1**	**2**	**3**	**4**	**5**	Staying within your budget (Proverbs 21:5)
Resentfulness	**1**	**2**	**3**	**4**	**5**	Gratitude (1 Thessalonians 5:16–18)
Apathy	**1**	**2**	**3**	**4**	**5**	Compassion (1 Peter 3:8)
Laziness	**1**	**2**	**3**	**4**	**5**	Productivity (1 Thessalonians 4:11–12)
Hopelessness	**1**	**2**	**3**	**4**	**5**	Courage (Isaiah 40:28–31)
Nastiness	**1**	**2**	**3**	**4**	**5**	Sense of humor (Proverbs 17:22)

2. In which of these areas is there room for improvement? Which areas will you choose to grow in during this deployment? How can you help your spouse grow?

Couple's Azimuth Check (40 minutes)

3. Share your answers from the chart in question 1.

4. What significant challenges have you faced as a couple?

5. The following is a list of some benefits that can come from struggles. Which of these benefits have you received from the challenges you have already faced as a couple?

- Stronger relationship with God

- Ability to forgive

- Discernment and better decision making

- Self-discipline

- Compassion for others

- Gratitude for what we have

- Awareness of the benefit of friends

- Knowledge that we're not alone

- Desire to help others by sharing what we've learned in our struggles

6. List any other lessons you have learned from these challenges.

7. During the group session we talked about five key attributes of couples who thrive during deployment. Talk about how you can apply those keys in your marriage and in this deployment.

Key #1: Couples who thrive are growing.

How does each of you plan to grow in maturity during this deployment?

Key #2: Couples who thrive are in a community.

What groups will you join to help you thrive during this deployment?

Key #3: *Couples who thrive have faith in God.*

What can you do to grow spiritually during deployment? How will your local chapel or church help you grow in your faith?

Key #4: *Couples who thrive understand that God is in control.*

Reflect again on Genesis 50:20, Isaiah 43:1–3a, and Romans 8:28. Recall an incident that looked impossible but turned out for the best.

Key #5: *Couples who thrive make God the anchor of their lives.*

Refer to the History Nugget. Can you share Jeff Struecker's confidence in the face of adversity? Why or why not? What are some ways you can develop your relationship with God? If you have questions, refer to appendix A on page 103.

Recommended Resources

Footsteps of the Faithful: Victorious Living and the Military Life, by Denise McColl

Calm My Anxious Heart: A Woman's Guide to Finding Contentment, by Linda Dillow

Lord, Change My Attitude: Before It's Too Late, by James MacDonald

Loving Your Military Man: A Study for Women Based on Philippians 4:8, by Beatrice Fishback

The Road to Unafraid: How the Army's Top Ranger Faced Fear and Found Courage Through Black Hawk Down and Beyond, by Jeff Struecker

Psalm 91: God's Shield of Protection, by Peggy Joyce Ruth

Web-based and Telephone Resources

Protestant Women of the Chapel: *PWOConline. org*. PWOC provides fellowship, Bible studies, and conferences on military installations.

Military Ministry: *MilitaryMinistry.org/Families*

American Association of Christian Counselors: *AACC.net*, 800-526-8673

- Christian Care Network—Locate Christian treatment in your area

- Treatment Centers—Locate Christian treatment centers

National Suicide Hotline: 800-273-8255

New Life Ministries: 800-NEWLIFE (639-5433)

- Nation's largest faith-based broadcast, counseling, and treatment ministry

Samaritan Counseling: *Samaritan-Center.org*, 512-451-7337

- Provides counseling for military who have served in Iraq and Afghanistan

Christian Counselor Directories:

- ChristianTherapist.com

- FindChristianCounselor.com

Focus on the Family: 719-531-3400, ext. 7700, or ask for the Counseling Department

Smoothing the Return Home

Demonstrating patience and grace toward one another will help optimize a joyful reunion.

History Nugget

I can't wait to be home to be with all of you. You can't begin to fathom—cannot begin to even glimpse the enormity—of the changes I have and am continuing to undergo. God takes you to the depths of your being—until you are at rock bottom—and then, if you turn to Him with utter and blind faith, and resolve in your heart and mind to walk only with Him and toward Him, picks you up by your bootstraps and leads you home ... I am at peace ... There is something far beyond my level of human understanding or comprehension going on here, some forging of metal through fire.[1]

—NBC journalist David Bloom e-mails his family from Iraq

1. Share something you learned during your HomeBuilders Project.

2. If you compared deployment to an airline flight, with a takeoff (pre-deployment), en route segment (deployment), and landing (reintegration), what would a smooth landing look like to you?

3. What would a bumpy landing look like?

CASE STUDY

You have the opportunity to introduce your neighbor, Maria, to another wife in the neighborhood, Sandi. Sandi's husband, James, has recently returned from a lengthy and demanding deployment. When Sandi learns that Maria's husband is about to deploy, she provides her own observation.

"Getting back together has been a real struggle," she says. "Perhaps I expected too much." She says that when James returned, the first two weeks seemed like another honeymoon. But then they started to have conflict.

Sandi says she was much different from the wife he had left behind. "I was more confident in my ability to handle the everyday challenges of the house, the children, and finances. James didn't know how to deal with that—his role as a husband and a father seemed different. The kids didn't respond to his authority the way he expected." (To be continued)

1. In what ways can you relate to James and Sandi's story? If you've been on a deployment, how was your reintegration?

Reintegration is not just reunion. It's the process of "feeling at home" again. It takes time and generally follows these five phases:

- A pre-return period—when service members prepare to come home (a busy time full of anticipation and excitement).

- A "honeymoon period"—the first few days when you are reunited with loved ones and celebrate coming home.

- A period of disruption—problems may surface if some expectations of "getting back to normal" go unmet in your relationships, work life, or other areas.

- An adjustment period—new routines, roles, and goals are negotiated in your family and personal life, and at work.

- An acceptance—embracing and appreciating all the things your "new" life offers.

Whether you were deployed or at home, you have been living in a high-stress environment.

Transitions have to be made. Everyone has changed because of the challenges and demands of the time apart.

Looking at the "New Normal"

We all change over time—no matter what the circumstances. Change is not a bad thing ... and it can be very good if you have matured as a couple. Couples need to understand that routines and responsibilities will be different from before—there will be a "new normal." Things will never be the same, but with God's help they can be even better!

2. As a group, list first your expectations and then your fears over reintegration.

3. Which of the following could be areas of conflict as you deal with the new normal during reintegration? (Or, if you've experienced a deployment, which of these areas led to conflict?)

Finances

Who is in charge

Use of free time

Use of block leave time

New friends/relationships

Visits with in-laws

Schedules (new routines)

Other

4. Having identified vulnerable areas in question 3, what plans can couples make before the deployment to smooth these adjustments? Draw from the experiences of other couples you believe have handled reintegration well.

Looking at Relationships

When armed forces personnel deploy as a unit, camaraderie and commitment to one another are essential for the unit's success. At home, there are support groups and coping routines that become very important to the at-home spouse. Building your spouse's needs back into your daily routine requires adjustments and unselfishness. This is a time when a couple really needs to look carefully at the words of Colossians 3:12–15:

> *Therefore, as God's chosen people, holy and dearly loved, clothe yourselves with compassion, kindness, humility, gentleness and patience. Bear*

with each other and forgive whatever grievances you may have against one another. Forgive as the Lord forgave you. And over all these virtues put on love, which binds them all together in perfect unity. Let the peace of Christ rule in your hearts, since as members of one body you were called to peace. And be thankful. (NIV)

5. Followers of Jesus Christ seek to act like Him in everything they do. Demonstrating compassion, kindness, humility, gentleness, and patience are Christlike qualities. As a couple, pick one of these qualities. Tell how you would like to demonstrate it to your spouse when you are reintegrating as a couple. Share your answer with the group.

Looking Out for Each Other

CASE STUDY (continued)

Sandi also said James had changed when he returned home from deployment. He became very distant, had problems sleeping, and displayed bursts of anger that were not in character for him.

"I know he had some tough times, but I couldn't understand why he couldn't just 'get over it,'" she said. "Now we have both come to understand that these are some of the symptoms of combat trauma."

Some service members come home wounded in ways that are not readily visible. It is important that we understand this and take this opportunity to seriously look at combat trauma.

"Combat trauma, or deployment-related stress," describes a spectrum of behavior observed in those who have been exposed to a traumatic combat-related event (or series of events) that involves actual or threatened death or serious injury and causes an emotional reaction involving intense fear, panic, helplessness, or horror. This results in:

- *Persistent re-experiencing of the event(s) through nightmares, intrusive thoughts, or dissociative episodes*

- *Obsessive avoidance of any stimuli associated with the event(s)*

- *Feeling "keyed-up" (aroused, angry, sleepless, jumpy) at all times*

The following continuum presents the spectrum of combat trauma:

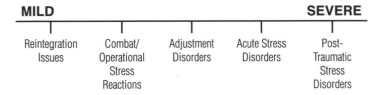

MILD				SEVERE
Reintegration Issues	Combat/ Operational Stress Reactions	Adjustment Disorders	Acute Stress Disorders	Post-Traumatic Stress Disorders

Combat Trauma sufferers toward the left end of the spectrum will usually exhibit fewer symptoms and they typically will improve without significant treatment. Sufferers at the other end of the spectrum exhibit profound symptoms which will persist for at least a month, maybe years, and—if untreated—a lifetime. These symptoms may not begin to surface for months or years after the traumatic event(s).[2]

—Rev. Chris Adsit
Combat Trauma Healing Manual

6. Refer to the diagram above. Where do you see James (from the Case Study) on this continuum? Why?

7. If you are Sandi's friend, what steps would you take to encourage her to help James in his readjustment?

8. Galatians 6:2 tells us, "Carry each other's burdens, and in this way you will fulfill the law of Christ" (NIV). During deployment, how can you look after your "battle buddy"? If you are the spouse staying at home, how can you look out for your neighbor who may be struggling with deployment?

9. First Peter 5:10 says, "After you have suffered for a little while, the God of all grace, who called you to His eternal glory in Christ, will Himself perfect, confirm, strengthen and establish you." Who is the Healer (in this Scripture verse)? How do you think God can restore someone who has experienced combat trauma?

10. Experience has shown that a pre-deployment discipline of prayer helps to minimize the post-trauma paralysis of communication that can further complicate a couple's healing process. Given your new awareness of combat trauma, review your action statement on prayer, which you developed for your deployment plan on page 29. Make changes as appropriate.

W R A P • U P   15   M I N U T E S

Answer these questions with your spouse and then share your answers with the group.

1. Read Romans 5:1–5:

Therefore, having been justified by faith, we have peace with God through our Lord Jesus Christ, through whom also we have obtained our introduction by faith into this grace in which we stand; and we exult in hope of the glory of God. And not only this, but we also exult in our tribulations, knowing that tribulation brings about perseverance; and perseverance, proven character; and proven character, hope; and hope does not disappoint, because the love of God has been poured out within our hearts through the Holy Spirit who was given to us.

What does this passage say about what we gain through perseverance? How would you apply this to the challenges you experience during reintegration? Refer to the History Nugget. What changes did the tribulation of war bring to the life of David Bloom? Were the changes positive or negative?

2. If another deployment comes along—or if you have the chance to advise another couple—what suggestions would you have about reintegration?

Make a Date

Our date is scheduled for—

_____
DATE

_____
TIME

_____
LOCATION

_____

| HOMEBUILDERS PROJECT | | 60 MINUTES |

Individually (15 minutes)

All of us want our homes to be peaceful and loving. For our homes to be like that, we need to individually be at peace and able to love with grace. This is possible when we walk in the power of the Holy Spirit—continually confessing our sins to God and asking Him to live His life through us. When we walk with Him, He provides the fruit of "love, joy, peace, patience, kindness, goodness, faithfulness, gentleness, self-control" (Galatians 5:22b–23a). If Christ rules in our hearts, He will rule in our actions.

Review the following table. Circle a number on each scale of 1 to 5 (poor to great) to indicate how well you demonstrate these fruits of the Spirit toward your spouse. Then write down one thing you could do to further demonstrate each of these fruits of the Spirit to your spouse.

Fruit of the Spirit	How am I doing?	My spouse will see this trait more in me if I ...
Love	1 2 3 4 5	
Joy	1 2 3 4 5	
Peace	1 2 3 4 5	

Fruit of the Spirit	How am I doing?	My spouse will see this trait more in me if I ...
Patience	1 2 3 4 5	
Kindness	1 2 3 4 5	
Goodness	1 2 3 4 5	
Faithful-ness	1 2 3 4 5	
Gentleness	1 2 3 4 5	
Self-control	1 2 3 4 5	

Couple's Azimuth Check (30 minutes)

1. Share with each other what you wrote down during your individual time.

2. What kind of difference do you think demonstrating these qualities will make in your home?

3. Are you willing to ask for or extend forgiveness if needed? (Refer back to "The Seven A's of Confession" on page 47, to help you answer this question.)

Individually (15 minutes)

4. Underlying a smooth takeoff, a smooth flight, and a smooth landing in deployment is an attitude of gratitude for the journey you are on together. Review your letter of appreciation from the HomeBuilders Project of session 3 and see if there is anything you would like to change or add.

Interact as a Couple

Once you have completed your letters, exchange them with one another.

Recommended Resources

American Association of Christian Counselors (*aacc.org*)

Down Range: To Iraq and Back, by Bridget C. Cantrell, Ph.D., and Chuck Dean

Life After Deployment: Military Families Share Reunion Stories and Advice, by Karen Pavlicin

The Combat Trauma Healing Manual: Christ-Centered Solutions for Combat Trauma, by the Reverend Chris Adsit

The Five Languages of Apology: How to Experience Healing in All Your Relationships, by Gary Chapman and Jennifer Thomas

Torn Asunder: Recovering from an Extramarital Affair, by Dave Carder

Reaching the High Ground of a Godly Legacy

Believing in God's purposes and applying
God's principles will strengthen your
marriage and ensure a godly legacy.

History Nugget

In the book of Psalms we find this passage written
by David, one of the greatest military leaders of
all time, a man of great courage and Israel's most
powerful king. It reflects a heart of confidence and
perspective in the midst of adversity:

> *The LORD is my shepherd, I shall not want. He
> makes me lie down in green pastures; He leads
> me beside quiet waters. He restores my soul; He
> guides me in the paths of righteousness for His
> name's sake. Even though I walk through the
> valley of the shadow of death, I fear no evil, for
> You are with me; Your rod and Your staff, they
> comfort me. You prepare a table before me in the
> presence of my enemies; You have anointed my*

*head with oil; my cup overflows. Surely goodness
and lovingkindness will follow me all the days of
my life, and I will dwell in the house of the LORD
forever.*

—Psalm 23

WARM•UP   15   MINUTES

1. Share something you learned from the
HomeBuilders Project.

2. Since this is the last session of the study, take a
few moments to share what the group has meant to
you. What have you learned from this experience?
How has it affected your marriage?

CASE STUDY

Al and Maria have benefited from their discussions with you and the other couples. Furthermore, they have taken the lessons from others to heart. They have had an "ah-ha" moment and have determined they will apply themselves, so their first deployment can be a successful one. What if their marriage is about more than just the two of them? They are beginning to understand the positive legacy that is possible when a military couple grows deeper in their marriage during deployment.

Like you, they are learning that deployment and reintegration will only be one of many trials faced in marriage. The fact is that trials only magnify the strengths and weaknesses that already exist in the relationship. If a couple experiences problems in their marriage, a deployment can make them worse. But if they have a strong marriage, with a strong foundation, they have a much better chance of thriving before, during, and after deployment.

1. From what you've learned in this study, and also from what you've observed in life, what would you say is the difference between God's way and the world's way in building a marriage?

There are two contrasting options by which to pattern our marriages and lives—God's way and the world's way. With the world's pattern, marriage is a 50/50 contract, where each person says they'll put an equal amount of effort into the relationship. However, this 50/50 relationship is easily undermined by our natural selfishness—we become concerned with having our own needs met and begin to regulate our effort according to our perception of our spouse's effort. The underlying mindset is: "As my spouse, you are to meet my needs and make me happy. I'm only obligated to continue meeting your needs if you are meeting mine."

Contrast that with God's pattern, where "It's all about God." Our desire becomes to glorify Him by completing each other. We freely admit we are dependent on God for everything, and interdependent on each other in our marriages to establish oneness. In this relationship, we are not concerned about each person doing an equal share—we're each committed to doing everything possible to make the marriage work. It's a 100/100 marriage in a covenant, not a contract.

And here's the secret: When you work to connect with God and with each other, you have the opportunity to experience true oneness—the type that comes from spiritual intimacy. This is what makes a marriage truly strong enough to withstand the challenges of a deployment or anything else life throws at you.

Connecting Through the Word

2. Read Psalm 119:105:

Your word is a lamp to my feet and a light to my path.

How can Scripture serve as a lamp and a light in one's life?

3. Read John 6:35:

Jesus said to them, "I am the bread of life; he who comes to Me will not hunger, and he who believes in Me will never thirst."

Jesus speaks of Himself as "the bread of life." What are some practical ways couples can find nourishment and strength from God's Word on a regular basis?

4. Refer to Psalm 23 in the History Nugget. What perspective can you gain from David's psalm to give you strength for deployment?

Connecting Through Prayer

Praying should include praise to God for who He is—His holiness and His attributes; confession of sin; thanksgiving for His provision, protection, and grace; and asking Him to provide for your needs and the needs of others.

5. Ephesians 6:18 tells us:

And pray in the Spirit on all occasions with all kinds of prayers and requests. With this in mind, be alert and always keep on praying for all the saints. (NIV)

Note how many times the word *all* is used in this verse. What do you think that means about praying?

6. How can praying with your spouse draw you closer together in your marriage relationship?

7. One of the best things you can do during a deployment is to pray together regularly. Here are some ideas for you to consider:

- Praying each morning and/or evening

- Closing your phone conversations, letters, or e-mails with prayer

- Keeping a journal of your prayers while you are apart and how they are answered

- Keeping a gratitude journal of what you are thankful for each day

- Other: _____

Turn to your spouse and ask how you can pray for him or her while you are apart.

Connecting Through Serving One Another

8. Philippians 2:3–4 calls us to serve each other in humility:

> *Do nothing from selfishness or empty conceit,*
> *but with humility of mind regard one another as*
> *more important than yourselves; do not merely*
> *look out for your own personal interests, but also*
> *for the interests of others.*

Turn to your spouse and discuss how you can serve each other during a deployment, even though you are not together. Share your answers with the group.

9. How could you serve others? How is serving others beneficial to you and to others, and honoring to God?

Connecting Through Worship

How do we learn these spiritual disciplines? Since we learn to walk by walking, to talk by talking, to write by writing, to teach by teaching, and to pray by praying, it follows we must learn to worship by worshipping! Some steps to learning to worship are prayer, singing, small-group Bible study, sharing how God is working in your life, having an attitude of submission to what God has planned for your life, and worshipping in a gathered body of Christ-followers, even in the desert.

10. What hymns or spiritual songs do you particularly enjoy? Is there a way to continue to enjoy this music during this deployment?

11. Why are small groups and corporate worship necessary for spiritual growth?

Connecting Through Love

12. What do the following verses say about the source of all love? How can you apply these passages to your marriage relationship?

We love, because He first loved us.

—1 John 4:19

God is love, and the one who abides in love abides in God, and God abides in him.

—1 John 4:16b

Jesus answered and said to him, "If anyone loves Me, he will keep My word; and My Father will love him, and We will come to him and make Our abode with him. He who does not love Me does not keep My words; and the word which you hear is not Mine, but the Father's who sent Me."

—John 14:23–24

"This is My commandment, that you love one another, just as I have loved you."

—John 15:12

W R A P • U P   15   M I N U T E S

Commitment Ceremony

The following ceremony is intended to be read aloud—ideally by a chaplain, pastor, or your group leader. However, if you are doing this study on your own as a couple, the husband should read the ceremony to his wife. There is an enhanced optional ending which includes a commitment certificate to be signed and a commitment coin as a keepsake. You may order the commitment coin and certificate from the Military Ministry online store at *http://resources.MilitaryMinistry.org.*

Leader should recite the following:

"First Corinthians 13 is one of the most beautiful passages of Scripture, and one of the greatest pieces of prose ever written about love:

> *If I speak with the tongues of men and of angels, but do not have love, I have become a noisy gong or a clanging cymbal.*
>
> *If I have the gift of prophecy, and know all mysteries and all knowledge; and if I have all faith, so as to remove mountains, but do not have love, I am nothing.*
>
> *And if I give all my possessions to feed the poor, and if I surrender my body to be burned, but do not have love, it profits me nothing,*
>
> *Love is patient, love is kind and is not jealous; love does not brag and is not arrogant, does not act unbecomingly; it does not seek its own, is not provoked, does not take into account a wrong suffered, does not rejoice in unrighteousness, but*

rejoices with the truth; bears all things, believes all things, hopes all things, endures all things.

Love never fails … . But now faith, hope, love, abide these three; but the greatest of these is love.

—1 Corinthians 13:1–8a, 13

"In these beautiful passages, we are challenged to think beyond ourselves to the most supreme gift we can give, and receive—love. Since this passage is read at so many weddings, it seems appropriate that we use it today as a reminder of the promise we made at our marriage ceremonies.

"We see what love is not: It isn't jealous, boastful, arrogant, selfish, or easily provoked. It does not hold grudges or celebrate unrighteousness.

"We see what love is: It is patient, it is kind, it rejoices in truth, it believes all things, hopes all things, endures all things … and it never fails.

"What kind of love is that—a love that could be all those wonderful, impossible things? That's God's love, and more than anything we are called to demonstrate to each other the love God showed us in the giving of His Son for our sin. When we learn to love in that selfless way, we will experience peace and joy that are truly gifts to savor in marriage.

"Our prayer is that this passage will be an inspiration to—and a description of—your marriage relationship. No matter what you face in life—a deployment or any other challenge—when you experience God's love, you can build the type of marriage that will stand strong.

"If you would now face your spouse and hold hands, recite as a couple the following commitment:

> Believing that God, in His wisdom and providence, has established marriage as a covenant relationship, a sacred and lifelong promise, reflecting our unconditional love for each other … and believing that God intends for the marriage covenant to reflect His promise to never leave us nor forsake us, we commit our lives to be faithful to each other during the unique challenges of military service and beyond … to seek God's help in order to finish strong, standing firm on the vows we made on our wedding day, and on the Word of God, which gives us the blueprint for this commitment."

The leader may then close the ceremony in prayer.

Optional Ending—Commitment Certificate and Coin

The leader should distribute the Commitment Certificates (one per couple):

"If you would now face your spouse and hold hands, recite as a couple the following commitment imprinted on your certificate: 'Believing that God, in His wisdom and providence, has established marriage as a covenant relationship, a sacred and lifelong promise, reflecting our unconditional love for each other ... and believing that God intends for the marriage covenant to reflect His promise to never leave us nor forsake us, we commit our lives to be faithful to each other during the unique challenges of military service and beyond ... to seek God's help in order to finish strong, standing firm on the vows we made on our wedding day, and on the Word of God, which gives us the blueprint for this commitment.'"

The leader should pass out the Commitment Coins (one per couple):

"If you look at this coin, you will notice that around the edge it reads: 'Love bears all things, believes all things, hopes all things, endures all things.' These are majestic phrases which mean that through Christ we can trust in the truth of God, through grace we can bear and endure seasonal suffering, and through faith we can live in hope for the future.

"You will notice that the heart comes out of the middle of the coin. Each of you completes the other—you are two halves who make a whole, and two wholes who fit together and create something even grander. Take this coin and remember how important you are to each other and how necessary you are to the oneness of your marriage. You may each take one part of the coin to be kept in a safe place during your deployment, and will put the two pieces back together when you are reunited.

"On the front of the heart it says, 'Love Never Fails.' May your love for each other never fail, just as Christ's love for us never fails.

"Before we close in prayer, take a moment now to sign your certificates and have another couple in the group sign as witnesses."

The leader may then close the ceremony in prayer.

HomeBuilders Principle
Developing your relationship with God will help you improve your relationship with your spouse.

Make a Date

Our date is scheduled for—

_____
DATE

_____
TIME

_____
LOCATION

HOMEBUILDERS PROJECT   6o   M I N U T E S

Individually (20 minutes)

1. Scripture tells us in 1 Corinthians 13 that love is patient and kind, is not boastful or proud, is not rude or selfish, is not easily angered, does not keep a record of wrongs, rejoices with truth, protects, trusts, hopes, perseveres, and never fails. How would you rate yourself in each of these qualities?

Kind words and actions

Humility

Forgiving

Trusting

Persevering

2. Ephesians 5:33 says, "Each one of you also must love his wife as he loves himself, and the wife must respect her husband." What are some practical examples of how you should treat your spouse?

3. Refer to the table (page 80) on the fruit of the Spirit. What changes do you need to make in order to make it easier for your spouse to love you or respect you?

Couple's Azimuth Check (40 minutes)

4. Share your answers to questions 1 through 3 with your spouse.

5. Agree on an action statement that would capture how you would improve the following commitments during deployment:

- Connecting through God's Word

- Connecting through prayer

- Connecting through serving each other

- Connecting through worship

- Connecting through love

6. Close the session by praying as a couple, using the following Scripture passage as a guide:

> *Who will separate us from the love of Christ? Will tribulation, or distress, or persecution, or famine, or nakedness, or peril, or sword?... But in all these things we overwhelmingly conquer through Him who loved us. For I am convinced that neither death, nor life, nor angels, nor principalities, nor things present, nor things to come, nor powers, nor height, nor depth, nor any other created thing, will be able to separate us from the love of God, which is in Christ Jesus our Lord.*
>
> —Romans 8:35, 37–39

Recommended Resources

Don't Waste Your Life, by John Piper

Infinite Impact: Making the Most of Your Place on God's Timeline, by Stu Weber

Rekindling the Romance, by Dennis and Barbara Rainey

FamilyLife.com

MilitaryMinistry.org

Connecting with God: Experiencing His Power

A mission plan requires power to implement it; otherwise the plan is useless. Likewise, if we are to implement the blueprints of marriage in accordance with God's Word, then we must have power. That power comes from a personal relationship with God.[1]

For those who seek it, God provides the power necessary to fulfill His purposes and to carry out His plan. We experience this power by knowing God and by allowing His Spirit to control our lives by faith.

1. God loves you and created you for a relationship with Him.

   a. God loves you.

> *"For God so loved the world, that He gave His only begotten Son, that whoever believes in Him shall not perish, but have eternal life."*
>
> —John 3:16

b. God wants you to know Him.

"This is eternal life, that they may know You, the only true God, and Jesus Christ whom You have sent."

—John 17:3

What prevents us from knowing God personally?

2. Humanity is separated from God and cannot know Him personally or experience His love and power.

a. All of us are sinful.

For all have sinned and fall short of the glory of God.

—Romans 3:23

b. Our sin separates us from God.

For the wages of sin is death ...

— Romans 6:23a

How can the gulf between God and man be bridged?

3. Jesus Christ is God's only provision for our sin. Through Him alone we can know God personally and experience His love.

a. God became a man in the Person of Jesus Christ.

The Word [Jesus] became flesh, and dwelt among us, and we saw His glory, glory as of the only begotten from the Father, full of grace and truth.

—John 1:14

b. He died in our place.

But God demonstrates His own love toward us, in that while we were yet sinners, Christ died for us.

—Romans 5:8

c. He rose from the dead.

*Christ died for our sins ... He was buried ...
He was raised on the third day according to the
Scriptures ... He appeared to Cephas [Peter], then
to the twelve. After that He appeared to more than
five hundred.*

—1 Corinthians 15:3–6

d. He is the only way to God.

*Jesus said to him, "I am the way, and the truth,
and the life; no one comes to the Father but
through Me."*

—John 14:6

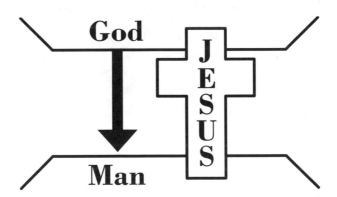

4. We must individually receive Jesus Christ as Savior and Lord; then we can know God personally and experience His love.

  a. We must change our minds about the way we have lived.

  b. We must receive Christ by accepting the free gift of salvation He offers us.

But as many as received Him, to them He gave the right to become children of God, even to those who believe in His name.

—John 1:12

For by grace you have been saved through faith; and that not of yourselves, it is the gift of God; not as a result of works, so that no one may boast.

—Ephesians 2:8–9

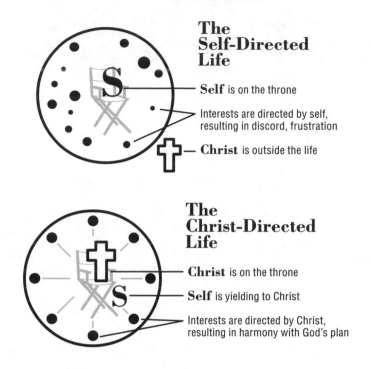

The Self-Directed Life

Self is on the throne

Interests are directed by self, resulting in discord, frustration

Christ is outside the life

The Christ-Directed Life

Christ is on the throne

Self is yielding to Christ

Interests are directed by Christ, resulting in harmony with God's plan

Which circle would you desire to represent your life?

5. What are the results of placing my faith in Jesus Christ? The Bible says:

a. My sins are forgiven (Colossians 2:13).

b. I possess the gift of eternal life.

And the testimony is this, that God has given us eternal life, and this life is in His Son.

—1 John 5:11

c. I have been given the Holy Spirit to empower me to pursue intimacy with God and oneness with my spouse.

6. I can respond to God right now by faith through prayer.

A suggested life-changing prayer: "Lord Jesus, I need You. Thank You for dying on the cross for my sins. I acknowledge that I am a sinner and I am separated from You. Please forgive me. I receive You as my Savior and Lord. Thank You for forgiving my sins and giving me eternal life. Please take control of my life. Make me the kind of person You want me to be."

SIGNATURE
_____

DATE
_____

Commitment Certificate and Coin

An engraved Commitment Certificate, suitable for framing, and the Commitment Coin, which comes in a gift case, are available for purchase. You may order the Commitment Certificate and Coin from the Military Ministry online store at *http://resources.MilitaryMinistry.org*.

Psalm 91
The Warrior's Psalm
True Then and True Now

*¹ He who dwells in the shelter of the Most High
will rest in the shadow of the Almighty.*

*² I will say of the LORD,
"He is my refuge and my fortress,
my God, in whom I trust."*

*³ Surely he will save you from the fowler's snare
and from the deadly pestilence.*

*⁴ He will cover you with his feathers,
and under his wings you will find refuge;
his faithfulness will be your shield and rampart.*

*⁵ You will not fear the terror of night,
nor the arrow that flies by day,*

*⁶ nor the pestilence that stalks in the darkness,
nor the plague that destroys at midday.*

*⁷ A thousand may fall at your side,
ten thousand at your right hand,
but it will not come near you.*

⁸ You will only observe with your eyes
and see the punishment of the wicked.

⁹ If you make the Most High your dwelling—
even the LORD, who is my refuge—

¹⁰ then no harm will befall you,
no disaster will come near your tent.

¹¹ For he will command his angels concerning you
to guard you in all your ways;

¹² they will lift you up in their hands,
so that you will not strike your foot against a stone.

¹³ You will tread upon the lion and the cobra;
you will trample the great lion and the serpent.

¹⁴ "Because he loves me," says the LORD,
"I will rescue him;
I will protect him, for he acknowledges my name.

¹⁵ He will call upon me, and I will answer him;
I will be with him in trouble,
I will deliver him and honor him.

¹⁶ With long life will I satisfy him
and show him my salvation." (NIV)

For thousands of years, this psalm has been an inspiration, comfort, and promise for warriors in harm's way. It is amazing to read the ancient descriptions of warfare described by the psalmist, and compare it to what we see in the global war on terror today. Insurgency, snipers, suicide bombers, IEDs, environmental terrorism—they seem to fit into the words "fowler's snare," "deadly pestilence," "terror of night," "arrow that flies by day," "pestilence that stalks in the darkness," and "plague that destroys at midday." What does God have to say in Psalm 91 that can calm our fears and help us to face the challenges?

Verse 1 begins with a great truth written in the third person—that he who dwells, or abides, in the shelter God provides will be resting in His shadow. The psalmist then makes this personal and speaks in the first person, stating clearly God is his refuge, his fortress, his God whom he trusts. This is a magnificent testimony!

The description of God's shelter in verse 4 is the image of God's wings which surround, cover, protect ... with His faithfulness as a shield. Within that bunker of strength the reader will be separated from the devastation around him. Is this physical protection or spiritual protection? We need both—

not just in our physical battles but also in the realm of spiritual battles.

Verse 9 begins with another great truth—he who makes God his dwelling will be protected. The statement of verse 1 now becomes the challenge of verse 9 with the word *if*. That is always the challenge ... and the choice. Will we choose to abide in the dwelling place of God?

If the reader chooses to allow God to be his shelter, as the psalmist proclaims he has done, then the Lord speaks the greatest truth of all in verses 14 through 16. He tenderly, yet powerfully, proclaims He will rescue those who love Him, who name His name. Our cries for help, in the form of prayer, He will answer, and His protection is sure even in the midst of battle.

And how does the Lord provide and protect? With His presence, His peace. We can trust His faithfulness knowing He loves us, has a plan for our lives, and desires us to live eternally with Him.

It is fitting that the psalmist ends this beautiful poem with the great truth, *"and show him my salvation."* Do you know His salvation? His salvation was provided by the ultimate warrior, Jesus Christ. Two thousand years ago, He faced the all-time champion of evil at Calvary and shed His blood in death on the cross for our victory. In the present we continue in battle with the enemy, but have Jesus' armor with which to stand and fight. And in the future day, He will return, fight the last battle, and reign victoriously over all the earth.

We, in this modern age, can personalize Psalm 91, this warrior's psalm, for ourselves. In any verse where you see the word "you" or "your," insert "me," "I," or "my." For example: "If [I] make the Most High [my] dwelling—even the Lord, who is [the psalmist's] refuge—then no harm will befall [me], no disaster will come near [my] tent. For He will command His angels concerning [me] to guard [me] in all [my] ways."

And to the loved ones at home or on the home front, you can personalize this psalm in order to pray for your dear one deployed in harm's way. Put his or her name where you read "you" or "your." For example: "Surely He will save [Name] from the fowler's snare and from the deadly pestilence. He will cover [Name] with His feathers, and under His wings [Name] will find refuge; His faithfulness will be [Name's] shield and rampart."

We invite you to take Jesus Christ as your Lord and Savior, and to personalize John 3:16 in declaration that you have believed and trusted in God and His Son, Jesus Christ: "For God so loved [me], that He gave His only Son, that if [I believe] in Him, [I] will never perish but have eternal life." When you make this declaration, you have made the decision to not only dwell in the shelter of the Lord, but to make Him your dwelling place for all of eternity.

Leaving a Legacy of an Enduring Marriage

Can you imagine a marriage journey that started 248 years ago, in the year 1760, and continues on to this day? Hard to believe, isn't it? But, we're not talking about just one marriage; rather, a legacy of enduring marriages from one special family.

Meet Morrie and Shirley Lawing. Morrie and his family can point to five generations of marriage from his family of origin—all those marriages going the distance and finishing strong.

You see, Morrie comes from an uninterrupted family history of stay-together marriages. All these couples were married more than forty years; and his grandparents, William and Lois, were married for an amazing sixty-two years!

I conclude from this truth a couple of things: First, it appears that lasting marriages beget lasting marriages. Secondly, a long marriage can also equate to a long life.

But what does it take to leave a legacy like this?

Morrie and Shirley Lawing, married forty-six years now, are volunteers with Military Ministry of Campus Crusade for Christ. Morrie is a thirty-year Air Force retiree and Vietnam veteran. He and Shirley speak around the country at Military Marriage seminars on a variety of installations.

When speaking to military couples, their presentations sparkle with humor, intrigue, and compelling personal stories of their life journey. A seasoned "everyman" and former lineman on his high school football team, Morrie still looks like he could knock you down at the line of scrimmage; his baritone voice grabs the attention of the audience. He speaks with authority when it comes to marriage—because he's been there.

When he addresses the importance of loving one's spouse, he pauses and levels his gaze at the wide-eyed audience of couples. Morrie begins to tell a story that was seared into his mind more than 35 years ago ... in Vietnam.

We had flown into Laos to establish a forward Base Camp. The military had sent 86 of us in to

establish the camp. Soon after arriving, we came
under heavy ground fire, which kept us pinned
down for over 26 days. The Viet Cong were using
RPGs, artillery, rockets, and whatever else they
could throw at us. We were under a constant
pounding day after day. During those 26 days,
help could not get to us due to the ground
firepower that ensued. Forty-nine members of
our group of 86 were killed, including my best
friend, George. George was hit in the chest with
an artillery round. Screaming for me, I ran out
to the compound to try and help. I put my hand
in the gaping hole of his chest trying to stop the
bleeding. As he was dying in my arms, his last
words were, "Tell my wife that I love her."

A best friend's dying words on a battlefield
are about his love for his wife. This memory
surrounded by the unspeakable horror of war would
occasionally, and unexpectedly, surface decades
later in a form of combat trauma known as Post-
Traumatic Stress Disorder (PTSD).

When Morrie escorted George's remains home, he
was able to pass on those last words to the man's
wife and family ... but those words continue to echo
in Morrie's mind. And they underscore the central
message he weaves throughout the seminars he
teaches—of building oneness in marriage.

Morrie and Shirley passionately speak about having a loving marriage that goes the distance. And when it comes to establishing a legacy of, say, 248 years of marriage, they insist it doesn't happen by accident.

At the end of our lives, there are four possible legacies we can leave:

- No legacy whatever

- A bad legacy

- A perishable legacy

- A godly legacy of destiny

The Lawings know what it means to have a godly legacy of destiny because they're living a life of hope and victory, even with the challenge of Morrie's PTSD.

Such a legacy can be summed up in two imperatives:

1. *Be committed.* Your steadfast commitment to Christ and each other will be the glue that keeps your marriage intact. Psalm 37:4–5 says, "Delight yourself in the Lord; and He will give you the desires of your heart. Commit your way to the Lord, trust also in Him, and He will do it." Maintaining a vertical (spiritual) and horizontal (relational) focus in your marriage will strengthen and nourish your relationship for a lifetime.

2. *Be persistent.* Yes, it's true that the toughest years in marriage normally come right after the wedding. Your commitment will be tested time and time again through trials and hardships, through changes in life, health issues, financial difficulties, professional disappointments, and even military deployments. James 1:2–4 says,

> *Consider it all joy, my brethren, when you encounter various trials, knowing that the testing of your faith produces endurance. And let endurance have its perfect result, so that you may be perfect and complete, lacking in nothing.*

Trials will make you either bitter or better. Don't let them drive you apart from your spouse and family.

Perhaps you have a family history of broken marriages. If you do, then you can join me by driving a stake in the ground and declaring a new legacy of destiny, so one day our great-great-grandchildren will rejoice in the longevity of our marriages.

Our legacy will be the everlasting impressions left behind for future generations. It will consist of a lifetime of memories our children and grandchildren will someday read and talk about.

Morrie says, "It's not so much about how you start the journey, but how you finish." May you finish your marriage journey well and have a legacy others will want to emulate.

Leader's Notes

Deployment Threats

Objectives

Deployment can bring many challenges to a military marriage. In this session, we call those challenges "threats" because if they are not properly addressed they will undermine the foundation of the marriage relationship.

In this session, couples will:

- Identify the deployment threats that can impact a military couple: uncertainties and difficult adjustments, selfishness, and poor communication

- Assess the impact those threats can have on military couples

- Share insights on how to positively address those challenges

Notes and Tips

1. A great resource for leading a Military HomeBuilders study like this is the *Discipleship Group Leader's Guide.*

2. If you have not already done so, you will want to read the "Notes to Group Leaders" information on page x in the introduction.

3. As part of the first session, you may want to review with the group some ground rules (see page ix in the introduction). These general rules are especially important for a group of military couples talking about deployment. Being sensitive to one another, and making the group comfortable, is key.

4. Because this is the first session, make a special point to tell the group about the importance of the HomeBuilders Project. Encourage each couple to make a date for a time before the next meeting to complete the project. Mention that you will ask about this during the Warm-Up of the next session.

5. Also because this is the first session, you may want to offer a closing prayer instead of asking others to pray aloud. Many people are uncomfortable praying in front of others, and unless you already know your group well, it may be wise to slowly venture into various methods of prayer. Regardless of how you decide to close, you should serve as a model.

6. You may want to remind the group during this opening session it's not too late to invite another couple to join the group. Challenge everyone to think about military couples they could invite to the next session.

Blueprints Commentary

Here is some additional information about various Blueprints questions. The numbers correspond to the Blueprints questions in the session. If you share any of this information in the discussion, be sure to do so in a manner that does not stifle discussion by making you the authority with the "real" answers. Begin your comments by saying something like, "One thing I notice in this passage is ..." or "I think another reason for this is ..."

Notes are not included for every question. Many of the questions in this study are designed for group members to draw from their own opinions and life experiences.

There may be a wide range of deployment experiences in your group. Discussing deployment can bring back memories of pain and disappointment. Be careful, be sensitive, and be understanding to those who may still be struggling. You'll want to focus on those who have positive experiences with deployment and have a spiritual perspective. This will serve to encourage the group as a whole.

1. Adjustments are hard and painful. Deployment simply makes marriage that much harder. Couples may struggle to identify and talk publicly about these adjustments. Be careful here not to personalize this topic too much. Ask how military couples address adjustments related to deployment.

4. Our attitudes, positive or negative, will certainly guide our emotional and spiritual well-being. Ask the experienced members of the group if they might share some personal development opportunities that occurred during their deployment period(s).

5. People do not like to consider themselves selfish. Ask the parents in the group how their children demonstrated selfishness when they were infants. Many will note that adults can behave in the same manner, by insisting on their own way. Marriage will not function well, and in fact, can fail when selfishness goes unchecked in a marriage relationship. Rather, marriage thrives when both act in a selfless way, as husband and wife look out for one another's best interests.

9. Because good communication is central to any marriage, the subject should come up in practically every session of the study. A healthy marriage will reflect transparent communication between husband and wife at all times, and for the military couple, during all phases of deployment: from pre-deployment through reunion and reintegration. Maintaining good communication is more challenging when the two of you are geographically separated.

—————————— **Session Two** ——————————

Mission Planning

Objectives

God's threefold plan for marriage is clear according to Genesis 2:24: "leave, be united, and become one flesh" (author's paraphrase). God's plan for marriage indicates a design, a "blueprint" for a successful marriage. Knowing there will be uncertainties and difficult adjustments ahead for a military couple facing deployment and developing a plan will help build unity and minimize stress.

In this session, couples will:

- Consider the meaning of "leave, be united, and become one flesh"

- Discuss the value of planning for important events in their lives

- Look at the different aspects of a deployment plan for their marriage and begin to develop it

Note and Tips

1. Since this is the second session, your group members have probably warmed up a bit to each other; however, they may not feel free to be completely open and honest about their marriage relationships. Don't force the issue, but continue encouraging couples to attend and to complete their projects.

2. You may wish to have extra study guides and Bibles for those who didn't bring theirs. Beginning with this session, there are numerous passages of Scripture in the study. Advance planning, such as handing out slips of paper with the Scripture references on them for selected members to look up before the discussion starts, will help you cover the material during the allotted hour and a half.

3. If someone joins the group for the first time this session, give a brief summary of the main points of session 1. Also, be sure to introduce those who do not know each other. You may want to have each new couple share their responses to the Warm-Up exercise in session 1.

4. Make sure any refreshments you're planning (not mandatory) have been taken care of.

5. If your group has decided to use a prayer list, make sure this is covered also.

6. If you told the group during the first session you'd be asking them to share something they learned from the first HomeBuilders Project, be sure to ask them. This is an important time for you to establish an environment of accountability.

7. This session's HomeBuilders Project includes an optional section, For Extra Impact, that encourages the couples to discuss the worst-case scenario for a deployment: death of a spouse. As you go through the Wrap-Up for session 2, consider a quick review of the HomeBuilders Project so you can mention this section and reassure the couples it is optional and not intended to scare or intimidate anyone. It is merely the reality of the dangers that come with the military profession. Couples who carefully and intentionally review these questions can better prepare themselves and their families for deployment.

8. For the closing prayer in this session, you may want to ask someone to close the group in prayer. Clear this ahead of time with this person, however, to make sure he or she is comfortable praying aloud in front of a group. Some people are not.

Blueprints Commentary

4. We tend to seek advice from people we trust, the "professionals," when it comes to planning our career, vacation, retirement, etc.). We do this because of their credentials and experience. We simply need help and often seek advice from those we can trust. In the context of the mission planning theme of this session, you'll want the group to see that they should seek advice from people who have experienced the challenges of keeping a marriage strong during deployment. And ultimately they should turn to God for help in developing a deployment plan.

6. The phrase, "leave, be united, and become one flesh" speaks to the physical, emotional, and spiritual dimensions of marriage. When a couple gets married, there should be a detachment from one's parents (physically, emotionally, and spiritually) followed by a similar three-dimensional uniting with the spouse. Be aware there may be some in the group who have not completely "left" their parents because of financial or emotional dependence. But also remember that some stay-behind spouses may choose to live with their parents during a deployment period. This does not mean they haven't left their parents in the context of this passage; it may simply be a matter of necessity during this time.

9. Through the long separation of deployment, it's very easy for couples to become so accustomed to operating apart and making decisions on their own that the sense of "us" is threatened. *Commitment* is the most important word in a military marriage, and it is severely tested during deployment. Couples need to work hard to ensure that they communicate, that they make important decisions together, and that they resist the temptation to make choices that would hurt their oneness and their dependence on each other.

Staying Connected with Each Other

Objectives

The title of this session speaks to the importance of couples communicating well with one another. Often in a military marriage, communication is strained because of the extraordinary demands placed on the family. This is particularly true during a deployment period in which the marriage-and-family paradigm begins to dramatically change.

In this session, couples will:

- Examine how listening, expressing, and resolving conflict can contribute to a healthy marriage relationship

- Identify statements that allow one another to share more deeply

- Talk about how resolving conflict can strengthen a marriage

- Develop a communication annex for the marriage deployment plan

Notes and Tips

1. Because this session will focus on communication, conflict, and forgiveness, it has the potential to make some uncomfortable. Therefore, approach the session carefully and with prayer.

Be careful on the issue of addressing unresolved conflict; watch out for a rising temperature in the group. Couples should understand that resolving conflict prior to the deployment would keep a marriage strong for its duration. Unresolved conflict will keep a marriage in a weakened state and possibly cause spouses to drift into isolation if it's not properly addressed.

2. Humor can lighten up the atmosphere during the Warm-Up period. As the facilitator, know how and when to use jokes and humorous illustrations to make a point while disarming some couples who may be closed, withdrawn, or angry.

3. Communication is the very life of a marriage. In marriage, nothing is as easy as talking; nothing is as difficult as communicating. Using words skillfully is an important part of communication, but even more important is that both husband and wife have a willingness to communicate in ways that result in deeper honesty and openness.

4. When a military couple finds out they're about to face deployment, it tests their communication skills in a major way. Typically, the deploying spouse will become consumed emotionally with getting ready to deploy with his or her unit. In fact, they "check out" mentally from their marriage and "check in" to their unit several months before the deployment. On the other hand, the mind of the stay-behind spouse becomes flooded with questions and concerns about their spouse, their immediate family, and the well-being of their children (if any). Consequently, it is easy for them to drift apart.

5. If a military couple's marriage is unhealthy, it may be because of communication problems or unresolved conflicts in the past. This session seeks to encourage couples and equip them with the tools to improve their communication skills. A marriage that reflects poor communication prior to deployment won't automatically get better over time. Therefore, a key objective for the HomeBuilders study is for the couple to be healthy prior to the deployment. With careful application of the principles from this study, the couple can achieve that objective.

Blueprints Commentary

4. Focus on understanding for a moment, because it's such an important part of communication. Be an active listener, not a selective one. The way to show interest in each other is to strive to understand what's going on in the other's life. Focused attention is remembering that the way your spouse feels may not be based on facts or reality. Be careful not to tell your spouse that his or her feelings are dumb or invalid.

7. Asking open-ended questions, as shown in the diagram, will communicate a genuine concern for and interest in your spouse. Do everything possible to communicate in a loving and sensitive way during the ramp-up to deployment. Emotions can be raw in this time period.

8. The three statements listed are examples of assumptions and a demand. These, along with questions that are too general, will stifle conversation. Also, giving one-word answers, such as "fine," can lead only to surface communication and preclude discussions of deeper feelings.

9. Talk about the advantages and disadvantages of each form of communication (e-mail, handwritten letters, phone calls/Webcam, etc.). This discussion is important because you'll be asking the couples to address this in greater detail in their HomeBuilders Project. Also talk about how to avoid just sharing facts and how to get into the emotional side of communication. Caution everyone that there may be some one-sided conversations at times and not to be alarmed if the e-mails or calls taper off, particularly around arrival in-country or during major operations. The spouse on deployment may not have access to communications or may not feel like or even be able to talk about what is going on around him or her.

12. Forgiveness is the safety net beneath every strong military marriage. Without the cleansing power of forgiveness, at best the marriage will be very hard duty. At worst it will be disaster. No matter how hard two people try to love and please each other, they will sometimes fail. With failure comes hurt. And the only ultimate relief for hurt is the soothing salve of forgiveness.

Talk about what forgiveness is. To *forgive* means "to give up resentment or the desire to punish." (*Webster's Dictionary*, 1979 edition) By an act of your will, you let the other person off the hook. Someone once said, "Marriage is the art of 24-hour forgiveness." We need to be willing to seek and grant forgiveness many times during the course of a military marriage.

Session Four

Thriving During Deployment

Objectives

Couples in the midst of deployment are also facing choices about how they'll manage during the separation period. Will they succeed, thrive, and grow ... or merely survive?

In this session, couples will:

- Examine the importance and influence of choices in one's life

- Consider the role that attitude has in the context of deployment

- Observe some positive aspects of deployment in marriage

- Be encouraged to make a commitment to Christ, who can empower them to thrive over the course of the deployment

Notes and Tips

1. Congratulations! With the completion of this session, you will be more than halfway through this study. It's time for a checkup: How are you feeling? How is the group doing? How is the study going? What has worked well so far? What things might you consider changing as you head into the second half?

2. This session can be the most transformational of the entire study because it addresses the importance of establishing a relationship with God through the person of Jesus Christ. Without this relationship, a couple will likely be facing an uphill battle throughout the deployment. With Christ and the careful application of biblical principles in their marriage, they will find hope, comfort, and strength to go the distance.

3. You may find some in your group who have not yet made a salvation decision. At some point during the session, a salvation testimony from a person or couple in the group could be very powerful in communicating hope to others who need it. If you decide to have a testimony shared, be sure to coordinate with the individual or couple at least a week in advance.

4. Point some to the gospel presentation in appendix A. Let them know that if they want to review God's plan of salvation with you or someone else, you're available to discuss it with them privately. Be sure not to put anyone on the spot or make them feel uncomfortable. Just because one of the unbelievers in the group does not respond affirmatively to the gospel message, it doesn't mean God is not working in his or her heart. So be patient and show grace to your group.

Blueprints Commentary

2-3. Our attitude will ultimately shape the way we see ourselves and the world around us. Consider the impact of spreading a small portion of Limburger cheese under your nose (Limburger cheese smells awful), then holding up a beautiful rose or some wonderful-smelling fragrance to your nose. Chances are you'll only be able to smell the cheese. That's how our attitude can affect others. For some, deployment is like sniffing Limburger cheese 24/7. And tragically, they'll blame their spouse and the military for the misery they're in. They need to have a new attitude and a new mindset. And this can only come through knowing God personally and then renewing and refreshing one's mind with Scripture, as seen in the following questions.

5. Ellie Kay's book, *Heroes at Home*, has some excellent, practical suggestions for how you can use deployment for personal growth.[1] These could trigger some good discussion:

Top Twelve Don'ts for At-Home Spouses:

- Don't have a negative attitude.

- Don't spend time alone with members of the opposite sex.

- Don't listen to your favorite love songs.

- Don't buy big-ticket items.

- Don't give in to impulse buying.

- Don't clean out your spouse's "stuff."

- Don't stay home alone.

- Don't turn down offers of help.

- Don't overdose on news shows.

- Don't overdo it on TV in general

- Don't use TV, videos, computers, or game systems as a baby-sitter.

- Don't list your physical address in the phone book or on any registration information.

Top Eight Do's for While They're Gone

- Do build something.

- Do enjoy the downtime.

- Do experience new adventures.

- Do spend time with extended family.

- Do exercise.

- Do become the new you.

- Do volunteer.

- Do give anonymous gifts.

See the book for a complete list and discussion; these are great ideas to ponder!

6. Being involved in a community is paramount. In fact, both the deploying and stay-behind spouses are encouraged to be plugged into a Christian community. The community of believers will provide guardrails when we feel ourselves begin to stray. They provide love, friendship, accountability, grace, mercy, and prayer support. If a couple is not connected to a community, they can be vulnerable to temptation and/or isolation.

Smoothing the Return Home

Objectives

Showing patience and grace during the reunion and reintegration period can help diffuse tension and strengthen the marriage relationship.

In this session, couples will:

- Explore the "new normal" in the relationship and recognize that change is not necessarily a bad thing, but a part of life's journey

- Recognize that having the right attitude, a Christlike attitude, can help address the challenges of uncertainties and difficult adjustments, selfishness, and poor communication during the reintegration time

- Consider that the reintegration period can be a time of rest, healing, and refreshment

- Examine how those who experience successful reintegration can help others who need encouragement

Notes and Tips

1. In this session, you will be addressing the subject of reintegration. It might be wise to remind group members not to share anything that would embarrass their spouse. The fact is that reintegration is where many couples fail. Communication problems, mixed emotions, unexpected changes and adjustments, financial hardships, etc., can cause many to give up in the marriage.

2. Reintegration can be stressful because you and your loved ones have gone through a period of change. Life after deployment involves adjusting to those changes and finding satisfaction in your new life. Reassure the group that it's absolutely normal to feel different emotions. They may feel joy and anticipation about returning home again; concern that their relationships with their loved ones may have changed; and unease, if they left behind any unresolved problems.

3. Again, a personal testimony may be appropriate from someone who's been there and can identify with these feelings ... and can provide hope and encouragement to the group.

4. Consider an extended time of prayer for this session. Ask for any volunteers who would like to share their need for prayer because of the difficult journey they've been on. Affirm and encourage them. Let them know that their prayer concerns are safe with the group.

Blueprint Commentary

4. Preparing for a smooth landing should speak to the importance of communicating well with one another. How will we respond to each other and the children during reunion? What are our plans and expectations? What might be our fears? How will we have all changed? What will the "new normal" look like? What should be the timing on reintegrating with the extended family? In other words, the more effectively you communicate before the landing, the smoother the landing will be and the less stress couples will experience. So, genuine communication and staying connected heart-to-heart as a couple are fundamental to successful reintegration.

8. We need "buddies" and "buddy couples" in our marriage. Married couples are generally under-encouraged. Small-group studies like this provide the encouragement we all need to sustain our relationships, grow spiritually, and be accountable to one another. Use this opportunity to promote continued involvement in HomeBuilders groups as a means for continued spiritual growth and marriage enrichment. Additionally, battle buddies can help with accountability because spouses tend to become more vulnerable to sexual temptation when they're separated from each other. Be sure to remind the group that battle buddies should be of the same gender, trustworthy, and reliable friends who are willing to help them guard their hearts and minds.

10. From PTSD observations, post-trauma communication between husband and wife is a central issue. A pre-trauma prayer ethic allows them to at least start where they left off, even if they are having great difficulty in talking directly and intimately with each other.

—————————— **Session Six** ——————————

Reaching the High Ground of a Godly Legacy

Objectives

Deployment and reintegration is a significant, part of a military couple's journey through life together. Careful and deliberate application of God's principles to the big picture of their marriage will strengthen their relationship to go the distance, finish well, and ensure a godly legacy.

In this session, couples will:

- Contrast the world's pattern versus God's plan for marriage

- Review the four ways to connect with God and with each other: prayer, serving one another, worship, and love

- Consider participating in a commitment ceremony—a public ceremony to rededicate their marriage to God and communicate their pledge to stay faithful to each other while deployed

Notes and Tips

1. This is the last session of the study. While this HomeBuilders Couples Series has great value, people are likely to gradually return to previous patterns of living unless they commit to a plan for carrying on with the progress made. During this final session, encourage couples to take specific steps beyond this series to keep their marriages growing. For example, you may want to challenge couples who developed the habit of a "date night" during the course of this study to continue this practice. Also, you may want the group to consider doing another study in the HomeBuilders Couples Series.

2. The lesson here is unique because it encourages couples to get up on the high ground of life and look beyond the deployment and reintegration. After all, marriage and life in general are so much bigger than military deployment. But sadly, negative experiences caused by deployment can cast a large shadow on a military marriage. The bottom line is that it's not about ourselves (note the first lesson about selfishness), but about God and living for Him. So the tools from this lesson are for equipping and encouraging couples to develop a loving, faithful walk with Him and with one another to build a legacy—one that truly goes the distance and impacts future generations.

3. A legacy of destiny is what every military couple should strive for. This legacy will be marked by three characteristics:

- Commitment—to the Lord and to each other

- Persistence—through the difficulties and trials,

because every couple will face them on their journey

- Application of God's principles—practicing love and forgiveness to sustain a marriage and become an example to others

The testimony of Morrie and Shirley Lawing (appendix D on page 119) is a good example of how this is true.

4. Talk about the fundamentals of the Christian life as important disciplines we should incorporate: prayer, attending church, reading the Bible and having a quiet time, and being involved in Christian community are essential dynamics to our growth and well-being as believers.

5. The commitment ceremony in the Wrap-Up of session 6 can be a powerful, inspirational event in a military marriage for those who are facing deployment. The session may be concluded with the commitment ceremony alone or by using the optional enhanced ending with the Commitment Certificate and Commitment Coin. You may order the Commitment Certificate and Coin from the Military Ministry online store at *http://resources.MilitaryMinistry.org*.

Blueprints Commentary

2. Talk about how God's Word is a bright light shining in a world of darkness. Quiet time (i.e., getting alone with God and reading the Bible) is a fundamental discipline of the Christian life we need to exercise to keep us walking in the light. In the Bible, we'll find daily counsel and encouragement as well as everlasting hope. Talk about the value of a quiet time in your own life.

4. You may get some comments on the History Nugget, which is Psalm 23. Some people may not understand it in this context, as a source of confidence in life. The only way they may have seen it used is in funerals.

5. Stress the overall significance of prayer in the life of a military couple. God's Word says to pray constantly. The single most important discipline a couple needs to learn is praying together as often as they possibly can. Prayer unites, heals, diffuses tension, draws husbands and wives together, and points them to Christ; and it can lead to supernatural things as God acts on those prayers. Nothing works better than prayer in addressing the needs of a military couple and their family.

10-11. Talk about what worship truly means. The heart of worship is surrender. Surrender evokes the unpleasant images of admitting defeat in battle, forfeiting a game, or yielding to a stronger opponent. It's not a term military people are comfortable with. But in this context, it means to give ourselves to Him, not out of fear or duty, but in love, "because He first loved us" (1 John 4:19). God simply wants all of our life, not just 95 percent. So offering ourselves up to God is what worship is all about. It means making Jesus our Lord, taking up our cross, dying to self, and yielding to the Spirit. Discuss the three barriers that block our total surrender to God: fear, pride, and confusion.

12. Talk about how love and commitment go together. We all made a commitment on our wedding day to love our spouse till the very end, for better or worse. The deployment period may test the love and commitment in a military marriage. That's where the strength idea comes in. We are weak, but He is strong! We find strength to love and remain committed to each other because we're trusting in Him. And He can be trusted!

The Next Step Is Multiplication

Congratulations on completing this study! We trust and pray that it has helped you strengthen your relationship with God as well as your relationship with your spouse. May your marriage continue to grow as you both submit your lives to God and live according to His blueprints.[1]

We encourage you to continue the small-group momentum by multiplying your study and generating new HomeBuilders studies called HomeBuilders discipleship groups (HBDGs). These are just like HomeBuilders, but intentionally focused on spiritual regeneration and multiplication. The Great Commission given by Jesus is clearly spelled out in Matthew 28:18–20, which says,

> *"All authority has been given to Me in heaven and on earth. Go therefore and make disciples of all the nations, baptizing them in the name of the Father and the Son and the Holy Spirit, teaching them to observe all that I commanded you; and lo, I am with you always, even to the end of the age."*

Making disciples, moving others to Christlikeness, is what HBDGs are all about and supports the Military Ministry goal of "transforming the world through the military of the world."

Our strategy for HBDGs is to use them to help propel growing spiritual movements in military communities, while meeting the felt needs of marriages and families. To illustrate our strategic vision, we have developed a four-phase model:

Phase I: MOBILIZE—Win men and women to Christ through evangelistic impact events. These would include Military Marriage or Parenting Seminars (see *MilitaryMinistry.org* for more information on these events).

Phase II: TRAIN—Build up and strengthen them in their faith through an HBDG.

Phase III: EQUIP—Disciple them using proven biblical tools for growth.

Phase IV: DEPLOY—Send them out as commissioned ambassadors who can lead and train others.

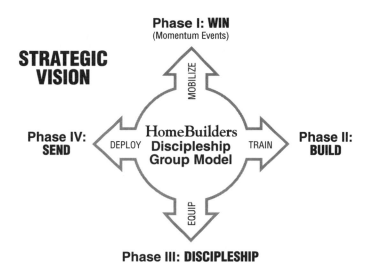

STRATEGIC VISION

Phase I: **WIN**
(Momentum Events)

MOBILIZE

Phase IV:
SEND

DEPLOY

HomeBuilders
**Discipleship
Group Model**

TRAIN

Phase II:
BUILD

EQUIP

Phase III: **DISCIPLESHIP**

Military people work with timelines and schedules. So Military Ministry has produced a conceptual timeline to offer you a visual aid on what your HBDG can look like. The timeline, a "12-Month Spiritual Battle Rhythm Plan," can easily be tailored to meet the needs of your group and circumstances. The key principle of multiplication, however, is an intentional focus of the group.

The leader must have a vision for identifying and challenging future HBDG leaders within the study. We recommend either using Campus Crusade for Christ's *Transferable Concepts* or *Your New Life in Christ* as a supplement to the HomeBuilders curriculum. The Battle Rhythm Plan is shown below; you'll notice two tracks: a HomeBuilders track to help couples grow in their marriage and a personal discipleship track that challenges individuals to grow in their personal walk with God.

12-MONTH SPIRITUAL BATTLE RHYTHM PLAN

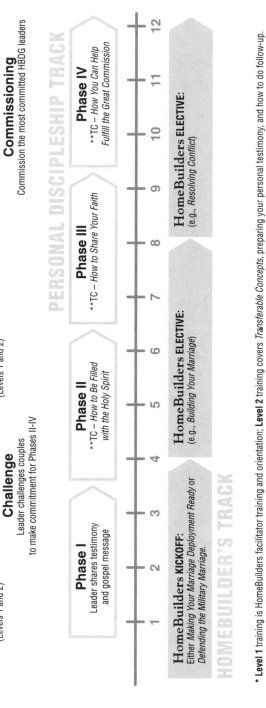

Momentum Event
*HomeBuilders Leader Training
(Levels 1 and 2)

Momentum Event
*HomeBuilders Leader Training
(Levels 1 and 2)

Challenge
Leader challenges couples
to make commitment for Phases II–IV

Commissioning
Commission the most committed HBDG leaders

PERSONAL DISCIPLESHIP TRACK

Phase I
Leader shares testimony
and gospel message

Phase II
**TC – How to Be Filled
with the Holy Spirit

Phase III
**TC – How to Share Your Faith

Phase IV
**TC – How You Can Help
Fulfill the Great Commission

1 2 3 4 5 6 7 8 9 10 11 12

HOMEBUILDER'S TRACK

HomeBuilders KICKOFF:
Either *Making Your Marriage Deployment Ready* or
Defending the Military Marriage.

HomeBuilders ELECTIVE:
(e.g., *Building Your Marriage*)

HomeBuilders ELECTIVE:
(e.g., *Resolving Conflict*)

* **Level 1** training is HomeBuilders facilitator training and orientation; **Level 2** training covers *Transferable Concepts*, preparing your personal testimony, and how to do follow-up.
** **TC** = *Transferable Concepts*. Another useful tool is *Your New Life in Christ* (also published by Campus Crusade for Christ).

To go deeper on HBDG, check *MilitaryMinistry.org* to order *HomeBuilders Discipleship Leader's Guide*.

Military Ministry— Come Join the Fight!

It is Military Ministry's honor and privilege to serve our troops and their families with spiritual support and the Word of God. We do this in many ways, but all focus is on the gospel because "it is the power of God for the salvation of everyone who believes" (Romans 1:16 NIV). With Paul, our "heart's desire and prayer to God for [military men, women, and families] is that they may be saved" (Romans 10:1 NIV). Only in this way will they be truly ready, spiritually ready, to face the challenges that will certainly come their way.

Please read about our ministries below and join us in prayer and in service to those who sacrificially give for us.

Your partner in the gospel,

Robert F. Dees
Major General, U.S. Army (Retired)
Executive Director, Military Ministry

The Six Strategic Objectives of Military Ministry

1. Evangelize and disciple enlisted service members at basic training bases and beyond.

> *My faith was nourished through your programs [at Lackland Air Force Base], and I will never forget what the Military Ministry did for me during that difficult time.*
>
> —Air Force recruit

Every Sunday, Military Ministry staff and volunteers lead Christian education classes at basic training and operational bases across America. Every week, hundreds make first-time decisions for Christ or openly renew their faith.

2. Develop Christian military leaders at service academies, ROTC campuses, and operational locations.

> *I came into Texas A&M as a "young" believer, and through my involvement in Military Ministry, I grew to understand foundational spiritual truths and how to apply them to my life and my mission.*
>
> —Army officer

Leadership makes a difference. Military Ministry offers spiritual nurture to future military leaders at service academies, ROTC campuses, and locations around the world—ships, flight lines, foxholes, and at special venues such as the Gettysburg Leadership Conference.

3. Stop the unraveling of the military family with conferences, support groups, spiritual resources, and leadership.

> *You brought us back from the brink ... now we are facing toward Christ instead of away.*
>
> —Military Marriage Seminar attendee

Divorce rates among military families are at epidemic proportions with repeated deployments and the normal challenges of military life taking their toll. The most vulnerable victims of family stress are military children.

Many of the solutions for maintaining family unity are spiritual in nature. We work to establish hope on the home front by giving families the faith and knowledge of Jesus Christ.

4. Arm troops in harm's way with spiritual resources.

The Bible in my Rapid Deployment Kit was the one I had, the only one. When we were reading our Bible … it was a big comfort … to read before missions.

—Soldier back from Iraq

I was overwhelmed at the demand for Military Ministry Rapid Deployment Kits.

—Chaplain

The Word of God has given millions of soldiers, sailors, airmen, Marines, and Coast Guardsmen the assurance of God's love as they encounter the toughest conditions our world can throw at them. Military Ministry teams work with chaplains and commanders to provide a spiritual resource network that troops and families can draw on during tough times. Our goals:

- A Bible in every "foxhole"

- Resources to support chaplains in every service of the Armed Forces

5. Wage global online evangelism, discipleship, and leader training.

I have received Christ in my heart and rededicated my life to Him … I want to grow and …

start my life off in the right direction.

—A visitor to *GodLovesAirmen.com*

Worldwide outreach to military members everywhere is now possible with the help of new technologies and partners. We are touching thousands of people with the gospel who might never visit a church or be available to hear the good news in person, but will surf the Web, even from deployment locations.

6. Change continents for Christ.

I can do my job much more effectively because of the Military Ministry in Kenya.

—Chief of chaplains, Kenya Armed Forces

Our vision is to see the militaries of the world lead their nations to Christ. The same strategic principles used in America apply to military ministry around the world. Working through indigenous military leaders, Military Ministry works to recruit, train, equip, and deploy military missionaries who will in turn build ministry teams in their countries.

Military Ministry Re-Supply

Help us get the word out about Military Ministry. Re-supply your efforts at *MilitaryMinistry.org* or by calling 1-800-444-6006.

- Prayer ministry—Submit prayer requests and learn how you can pray for our military.

- Bibles and spiritual development tools

  » Rapid Deployment Kits—A New Testament, daily devotional, and gospel presentation

  » Spiritual Fitness Kits—Discipleship tools for the new or growing believer

  » Family Readiness Kits—*Hope on the Home Front* inspiration for spouses and children

  » Chaplain's Boxes—A resource sampler for chaplains everywhere

- Post-Traumatic Stress Disorder (PTSD) resources—material for individuals and churches

  » *Bridges to Healing* DVD

  » Training curriculum

  » *Bridges to Healing* brochures

- *Standard Bearer*—The Military Ministry news source, online at *MilitaryMinistry.org/news/ standardbearer* or by mail

- Military Ministry brochures, videos, bulletin inserts

- Ambassador Kits—To help you tell churches or friends in your community about Military Ministry

Endnotes

Session One

1. Dwight D. Eisenhower, 1944. *Collection DDE-EPRE, 1916-1952*, National Archives.

2. Anne Borcherding, "Sharing My Calling," *Command of Officers Christian Fellowship* (April 2007)

Session Two

1. William Jones, *Christ in the Camp* (Harrisonburg: Sprinkle Publications, 1986), 134.

Session Three

1. Andrew Carroll, *Grace Under Fire* (Colorado Springs: Waterbrook Press, 2007), 34.

2. Carol Vandesteeg, *When Duty Calls*, (Colorado Springs: Cook Communications/Life Journey, 2005), 40.

3. Adapted from HomeBuilders: *Defending the Military Marriage* by Jim and Bea Fishback, (Little Rock: FamilyLife, 2005), 54.

4. *Weekend to Remember*, (Orlando: Campus Crusade for Christ, 2005), 179.

5. © Peacemaker Ministries. Used by permission. From *The Peacemaker: A Biblical Guide to Resolving Personal Conflict* (3rd Ed., Baker Books). *www.Peacemaker.net*

Session Four

1. Jeff Struecker, *Bullet Proof Faith*, 6.

Session Five

1. Andrew Carroll, *Grace Under Fire* (Colorado Springs: Waterbrook Press, 2007), 125.

2. Chris Adsit, *The Combat Trauma Healing Manual* (Newport News: Military Ministry Press, 2007), 22.

Appendix A

1. Adapted from Campus Crusade for Christ, s.v. *Have You Heard of the Four Spiritual Laws?*, *http://www.campuscrusade.com/fourlawseng.htm* (accessed September 10, 2008).

Appendix E

1. Ella Kay, *Heroes at Home* (Bloomington: Bethany House, 2002), 171-175. Used with permission.

Appendix F

1. Adapted from HomeBuilders: *Defending the Military Marriage* by Jim and Bea Fishback, (Little Rock: FamilyLife, 2005), 35.

Ways to serve those who serve ...

Please provide more information on:

- ☐ Prayer ministry
- ☐ Bibles for our troops
- ☐ PTSD-ministry for my church
- ☐ Military Marriage Seminars
- ☐ HomeBuilders groups for military couples
- ☐ International ministries

Other

Send me/us the *Standard Bearer* newsletter

- ☐ By e-mail to

E-MAIL ADDRESS

- ☐ By postal mail
- ☐ Other

I/we ...

- ☐ Will pray for the spiritual needs of military couples.
- ☐ Would like to volunteer our time to minister to military couples.

☐ Would like to provide a financial gift to Military Ministry.

» 1. To give online, visit *MilitaryMinistry.org* and select "Give Online."

» 2. For more information on support opportunities, e-mail *development@milmin.org*.

_____

NAME(S)

_____

E-MAIL ADDRESSES

_____

ADDRESS

_____

_____

CITY, STATE, ZIP

_____

PHONE INCLUDING AREA CODE

☐ Please call me.

Military Ministry
P.O. Box 120124
Newport News, VA 23612-0124

1-800-444-6006

E-mail: *info@milmin.org*

MilitaryMinistry.org

Combined Federal Campaign #12040

NOTES

NOTES

NOTES

NOTES